It Must Not Be Done So

Pitchou Khalala

It Must Not Be Done So

Copyright © 2020 by Pitchou Khalala

ISBN 978-1-7776772-0-6

The majority of quotes used in this book come from the New King James Version (NKJV) Bible, unless noted otherwise.

Contact us:

Praise24hours@gmail.com

Edited by:

StellarWork Editing
stellarwork.info
natasha@stellarwork.info

Cover design and page layout:

Jerry Mensah (J Mens Dreams Studios)
Jmens027@yahoo.com

TABLE OF CONTENTS

INTRODUCTION

This book was written to help you recognize the forces that stand in your way to block, restrict, resist and refrain you from being what you ought to be in this life.

God created you to live your own destiny; you are in this life not to copy the story of your parents, but to rewrite your own story for the generations to come.

In this book, we will look at certain phenomenal situations that delay us in life, even whilst we've come to the Lord and are saved, spirit filled, and speaking in tongues. The fact that you are a believer doesn't change the DNA of your biological parents, which means you are subject to the spiritual pattern of your family.

I remember reading a quote that read, "Heredity is stronger than demons," and the writer continued to state that, "environment is stronger than heredity."[1]

The title of this book, *It Must Not Be Done So*, is taken from Genesis, when Jacob, after fleeing from his brother's fierce anger, settled with his uncle, the brother of his mother. It seems that Laban was reluctant to break the customs of his family, which I will get into shortly.

Now why are customs so important? Our customs are our way of life. They include our values, beliefs, culture, languages and

---

[1] Wallace D. Wattles. *The Science of Getting Rich (Audiobook)*. Blackstone Audiobooks, 2018.

traditions. Customs are reflected in our history, our heritage, how we express our ideas and creativity, and the quality of our life.

Our customs measure our quality of life, our vitality and the health of our society. Through our customs we develop a sense of belonging, personal and cognitive growth, and the ability to empathize with and relate to each other. Direct benefits of a strong and vibrant culture include health and wellness, self-esteem, skill development, social capital, and economic return. The force of customs and traditions caused Jacob to spend 14 years of his life to get Rachel.

He sought to get married to the love of his life. He chose the woman that he wanted, but there was an issue that Jacob was not aware of. Jacob later found out that he got himself into a custom that did not allow the younger daughter's marriage to precede the older daughter's. So, regardless of his efforts and abilities, the customs and traditions had to be respected and followed. It was impossible to have the younger go before the first born. Nevertheless, Laban's act of switching girls during the honeymoon was not cool; however, emotions do not affect the spiritual world. What Jacob had to do was fight back persistently until the power of the customs no longer affected him. In reality, customs defeated Jacob, and he had to resort to serving for another seven years in order to get the woman he loved.

Rachel understood this very clearly, to the point that she never let go her household gods. This shows us that the customs and traditions of the people have a very significant bearing on the individual.

It is possible to be a believer and be bound by the patterns of the traditions and customs of your family. Remember, Rachel was bound to be second to her sister in life because of her people's customs. When I was writing this book, it dawned on me that Laban knew what was happening in the family, yet he gave Jacob hope that he was serving the first seven years for Rachel while it was really for Leah. Laban knew this all along.

When Jacob discovered that he was given another woman instead of the woman he wanted to marry, we discover that things got heated in that moment; Jacob was furious. However, consummation of the marriage had occurred and he had nothing to do than to serve for another seven years. *It must not be done so* in Laban's customs to give the younger daughter for marriage before the first born. Jacob was not there when this custom was instituted in the family, yet it affected him severely. That which he had worked so hard for was in vain.

We also saw that, when the sisters were in their marital home, the first born started having children whilst the younger's childbirth was delayed. The latter was bound to be second in life in everything due to tradition.

In this book, I will go in depth of some of the traditions and customs that have affected our lives. For example, most of us come from families where there is a strong establishment of witchcraft and sorcery. As a result, a lot of mysterious things happen that we could never explain. Even though we have come to know Jesus as our Lord and savior, we experience things that we cannot explain or tell anybody about. Sometimes we keep falling to a particular sin over and over again.

If I may ask you a question, what is it about your family that you do not understand?

Please don't just let things be, but ask the right questions in order to get to the root of the issues. Questions are important to get to revelation. If Jacob never confronted Laban, he would have accepted Leah; but instead he tried to give Laban what he asked for, even if it was not enough until he met with the angel of the Lord and things began to change over his life.

Until you lift up prayer nothing will change; if you do not have a prayer life, it will only be a matter of time until you are defeated. I do not want to get ahead of myself; so let's look at this first. Jesus said that no one can enter into a strongman's house unless he first binds him and plunders his goods (Marc 3:27). I want us to look at this in just few minutes please.

You may be asking, Jesus actually established a rule? What are you talking about pastor? As much as you must first bind the strongman before you take back what is yours, in the same manner he cannot get your life and your stuff unless he first binds you. It's a law that if you want to plunder, you must first bind the owner. Now imagine how many people have been bound and taken advantage of. The issue here is the word that was spoken – it must not be done so for your life. Until you rise up in prayer, you will just be like everyone doing the same things and being stuck in life. *That's why prayer is not just about shouting; it's about rising to the gates of eternity to change the course of your destiny*. Your future is brighter than you think, it's about time to take your destiny into your own hands and travail in prayer.

I want to tell you the story of how this book came to a reality. One day I was invited as a speaker to one of our church branches and after the Saturday night meeting, whilst I was in my hotel room something happened to me. God gave me a revelation; it dropped in my spirit like water dripping from the roof.

I came into my room and my spirit could not rest. I don't know if you have an idea of what I am referring to. As a preacher you have those moments when you get an inspiration from heaven knocking at the door of your spirit.

After the meeting I was invited to, my spirit was awake. I really cannot explain it fully in words. But as we finished church, I was driven to my hotel room and as soon as I got there, God just began to pour revelations into my spirit. It was almost like God wanted me to sit on that particular chair in that room, so that He would begin to pour out the abundance of His revelation upon me. The scriptures that I had read, studied, and preached from for some time, this time, deep exposition and extraordinary mysteries were revealed to me.

I want you to join me on the journey through this book. I feel like a pregnant woman that needs to deliver. There are a lot of things happening nowadays in the body of Christ, and most of us are just going through the motions without making our mark. As a minister of the gospel I have seen and experienced so many things, but that night in that hotel room I understood why I went through the troubles I had experienced in my personal life. At one point I asked

God a lot of questions. Now I get it. I have to step-up my prayer life to a level it has never been before in order to have the victory and be able to say that now, it *must be* done so, because I have wrestled, and prevailed in spiritual warfare prayer.

CHAPTER 1
Where it All Began

Quote: "Your prophecies do not replace your prayer life."
- Pastor PK

The story starts with Jacob. Jacob had been born from the family of Isaac, the son of Abraham, and he was born second to Esau. One day as Esau was coming back from hunting having caught nothing, he came home very hungry, while his brother, Jacob had cooked a soup that smelled so good. The aroma of the soup Esau could not resist, so he hurriedly asked his brother for some.

Esau asked Jacob for a portion, and Jacob took the opportunity to renegotiate a life business deal; he basically realized that the time to make a deal is when you have the command key in your hand.

One life lesson I have learned is to always learn to negotiate when you have the key of command in your hand. In Jacob's case, he realized that he had the power in his hands at that moment, so he said to himself, "let me strike a deal now." So Jacob offered a bowl of soup for a birth right.

If you look at it naturally, you can decide to judge Jacob, saying, "look here man; this is your brother," but he understood that for him to position himself in this life, and stand where God will not miss him, he needs this.

The transaction was approved by Esau. He said to Jacob, "I'm dying where would I take this birth right? (Genesis 27:1-6)" So, Jacob gave him the soup. My observation from this is: who told you that you are dying? How is it that you only target death as you had no food? Think about it!

Be careful of the type of deal you sign up for with your life. ***Do not let your life decisions sign you up on a deal that will jeopardize your entire destiny.***

Esau's mouth confession hooked him up with a deal which I strongly believe he wished he never got himself into. What type of life deal are your life decisions signing you up for? Your mouth has the ability to put your entire life in trouble. The tongue has a great deal of good and bad decisions tied to it that can easily affect us.

Jacob took the blessings of Esau and ran with them, because he had a deal with Esau. Old age had caught up with their father, Isaac and he could no longer see clearly. He called his son Esau and said to him, "I am about to die so hunt me a game make as I like and bring it to me, I'll eat it and my soul will bless you (Genesis 27:18-23)."

Esau left the presence of his father to do exactly what his father had requested, and while the father was talking to Esau, the mother Rebecca heard them speaking. So, she called Jacob, and told him about the blessing that was coming.

To abridge the story, Jacob found himself in front of his father; and in the midst of transferring the blessings his father said, I hear the voice of Jacob but the smell is the smell of my son Esau. The father asked him again are you really my son Esau? And the Bible says Jacob said yes and he blessed him there.

At this point Jacob received the blessing of his father. Let us look at the blessing of Jacob from his father very closely.

Genesis 27

> *²⁶ Then his father Isaac said to him, "Come near and kiss me, my son." ²⁷ So he came near and kissed him. And Isaac smelled the smell of his garments and blessed him and said, "See, the smell of my son is as the smell of a field that the LORD has blessed! ²⁸ May God give you of the dew of heaven and of the fatness of the earth and plenty of grain and wine.²⁹ Let peoples serve you, and nations bow down to you. Be lord over your brothers, and may your mother's sons bow down to you. Cursed be everyone who curses you, and blessed be everyone who blesses you!" (Genesis 27: 26-29)*

Verse 29 of Genesis 27 says, "Let peoples serve you and nations bow down to you."

Well, Jacob left the presence of his father and his brother came back, and the story continues. The reason I took time to tell this story is because I want us to understand the consequences of our decisions.

Genesis 28

So now in Chapter 28 of Genesis, the father blessed Jacob again without asking him why he did what he did to his brother, Esau. Let's look at the second blessing Jacob received from his father:

> *³ **God Almighty bless you and make you fruitful and multiply you, that you may become a company of peoples**. ⁴ May he give the blessing of Abraham to you and to your offspring with you,*

that you may take possession of the land of your sojourning's that God gave to Abraham!" [5] Thus Isaac sent Jacob away. And he went to Paddan-aram, to Laban, the son of Bethuel the Aramean, the brother of Rebekah, Jacob's and Esau's mother. (Genesis 28:3-5)

After this second blessing, the father sent Jacob to his uncle's house in Paddan-aram to be secured from Esau, who had decided to finish Jacob as soon as their father was dead.

When Isaac heard that his son, Esau was coming for his blessing, he realized he had been deceived by Jacob. But he couldn't give any blessing to Esau, and Esau was furious. The intensity of Esau's anger was so disturbing that it caused their mother, Rebekah to send Jacob to his uncle's house. At the advice of his mother, Jacob ran to his uncle's place. The first night of his journey he slept and saw the heavens open, with angels ascending and descending.

Let's read it in Genesis 28, from verse 10:

[10] Jacob left Beersheba and went toward Haran. [11] And he came to a certain place and stayed there that night, because the sun had set. Taking one of the stones of the place, he put it under his head and lay down in that place to sleep. [12] And he dreamed, and behold, there was a ladder[b] set up on the earth, and the top of it reached to heaven. And behold, the angels of God were ascending and descending on it! [13] And behold, the LORD stood above it[c] and said, "I am the LORD, the God of Abraham your father and the God of Isaac. The land on which you lie I will give to you and to your offspring. [14] Your offspring shall be like the dust of the earth, and you shall spread abroad to the west and to the east and to the north and to the south, and in you and your offspring shall all the families of the earth be blessed. [15] Behold, I am with you

and will keep you wherever you go, and will bring you back to this land. For I will not leave you until I have done what I have promised you." [16] *Then Jacob awoke from his sleep and said, "Surely the LORD is in this place, and I did not know it."* [17] *And he was afraid and said, "How awesome is this place! This is none other than the house of God, and this is the gate of heaven."*

[18] *So early in the morning Jacob took the stone that he had put under his head and set it up for a pillar and poured oil on the top of it.* [19] *He called the name of that place Bethel, but the name of the city was Luz at the first.* [20] *Then Jacob made a vow, saying, "If God will be with me and will keep me in this way that I go, and will give me bread to eat and clothing to wear,* [21] *so that I come again to my father's house in peace, then the LORD shall be my God,* [22] *and this stone, which I have set up for a pillar, shall be God's house. And of all that you give me I will give a full tenth to you."* (Genesis 28: 10-22)

After all these confirmations and reaffirmations, you would think that Jacob's life would be a smooth sail into his destiny. But instead, this marked the beginning of his trouble until Genesis, chapter 32, when he remained alone and a man wrestled with him. ***Many people believe if God said it, then that settles it – what a lie. You must fight to see what God has said about your life.***

Until you wrestle nothing will change, because to wrestle is the only option for your life to see the light of the day. Let's see what it means to wrestle.

According to the Webster online dictionary[2] definition, to wrestle is: *to take part in a fight, either as a sport or in earnest, that involves grappling with one's opponent and trying to throw or force them to the ground.*

It's very important to comprehend the definition of wrestling because it will serve us to establish certain points later on.

What you have to know is that the purpose of wrestling is *to gain control over the opponent so that they give up or abandon the fight.*

We see this on wrestling shows, whereby an opponent throws the other opponent on the floor and overpowers them until they abandon or give up. The main job of the devil is to frustrate you until you abandon and give up in life. Too many people have given up, abandoned and are just living, going through life purposelessly.

You've got to understand that is the main job of your enemy, the devil, to the point that you abandon and give up in life. He does not care if you are a Christian or go to church; he still wants to fight against you. The Apostle Paul when talking to the Ephesians reveal to them in Chapter 6 that we do not wrestle against flesh and blood, but against principalities, powers, rulers of darkness and against wicked spirits of this age.

He was not addressing the unbelievers if you can bear it, but the believers. His letter was to the church, so we've got to be very careful

---

[2] Merriam-Webster.com, s.v. "wrestle," accessed May 20, 2018, https://www.merriam-webster.com/dictionary/wrestle

not to be ignorant and let the devil gain advantage over us and frustrate us to the point that we give up in life.

Let me tell you about a dream I had when we started our church in the city of Montréal, Québec. In the dream I had come back from a trip and was going to church, as it is my habit after every trip to go to the altar inside the church to kneel down and thank God for everything He had done for me during the ministry trip I was on.

As I was approaching the church, I saw in the dream that all the lights of the church were left on, plus the person who had the keys to the church was someone that was not a member. I saw that individual going down the street. I rushed to the church in the dream to switch off the lights because of the cost of electricity. As I was there in the church, I saw that everyone had left to go home; however, a couple was living there and they had a dog, a dark and ugly dog.

I confronted them and cast them out of the church sanctuary, as these beings were very dark and short, and they had tried to attack me; but I threw them out of the sanctuary. I followed the man who had our church keys, and he started running away since I had discovered that he had the church keys while he was not even a member or a leader in the church.

I can tell you that before this revelation of the Spirit of God, the state of our church was spiritually struggling in ministry. People came and people left, and the attendance remained the same – our growth was stagnant. I didn't enjoy the presence of God, because the church seemed to be just very dry; we were not experiencing the dynamic move of God. Our worship was mechanical and the church commitment was not there.

This is my story prior to this dream, and every prophet we invited told us about what God was about to do with the ministry and all the great messages that would come out of it. It was only after the revelation in my dream that I really woke up and understood the depth of what I was facing in ministry.

Let me now get back to the story of Isaac. So Isaac sent Jacob to his uncle's house to keep him away from trouble with his brother; but one thing Isaac ignored was the spiritual troubles. *You can move away from physical battle to avoid confrontations but you can never move away from spiritual battles until you face and confront them.*

Some people are facing their spiritual confrontation in their native country and some away from their native country.
I want you to keep on meditating on the blessings of Jacob for a while and see how great those blessings are.

When the Lord releases a prophetic word over our life, the Heavens tell us His will and it is relevant.

While Jesus was teaching His disciples to pray in Matthew 6:10, He said, *"Your kingdom come, Your will be done."*

It is one thing to receive a prophetic word for your life, and it another thing to see it happen in your life.

Hear me very well; God is not responsible after you receive a word from Him. You have the definite responsibility to make that word happen in your life.

As much as I want to continue writing, let me conclude this point by saying this: after you have received all the words Heaven has for you, *now you must deal with the forces of opposition that are mandated to opposed you intentionally.*

Do you have any idea of the type of opposition that you face in life? God's word comes into our lives to take us beyond physical and spiritual limitations that stand in our way. It is significantly important to begin to see the type of opposition you face in life; we will look at this in detail in the next chapter. However, before I end this chapter I want to give you a few things to think about:

- Do you know the type of blessings that rest over your life?
- Having the prophecies is good, but Apostle Paul said to Timothy to wage warfare according to the prophesies once released over you (1 Timothy 1:18-20).
- You are responsible for the manifestation of what God has declared over your life.
- **Engage to confront**: you must engage to confront so that your life will make sense.

CHAPTER 2
Laban Says it Must Not Be Done So

Quote: *"If your enemies enchant your name more than you call on the name of your God, it will be only a matter of time they will overcome you."*

- Archbishop Duncan Williams

Let me continue with the story of Jacob and Esau. After Jacob had a dream and woke up in the morning, he anointed the stone he was sleeping on. I remember I preached a message on this passage when I was transferred to Quebec City when I used to work for an organization; that day something happened in the church.

Now Jacob got to his destination, to his uncle's place, and stopped by the well. The bible says that He saw Rachel. Let us just read it again, please, in the book of Genesis.

Genesis 29

> *⁹ While he was still speaking with them, Rachel came with her father's sheep, for she was a shepherdess. ¹⁰ When Jacob saw Rachel the daughter of Laban his mother's brother, and the sheep of Laban his mother's brother, Jacob went up and rolled the stone from the mouth of the well and watered the flock of Laban his mother's brother. ¹¹ Then Jacob kissed Rachel, and lifted his voice and wept. ¹² Jacob told Rachel that he was a relative of her father and that he was Rebekah's son, and she ran and told her father.*
>
> *¹³ So when Laban heard the news of Jacob his sister's son, he ran to meet him, and embraced him and kissed him and brought him*

to his house. Then he related to Laban all these things. ¹⁴ Laban said to him, "Surely you are my bone and my flesh." And he stayed with him a month.

¹⁵ Then Laban said to Jacob, "Because you are my relative, should you therefore serve me for nothing? Tell me, what shall your wages be?" ¹⁶ Now Laban had two daughters; the name of the older was Leah, and the name of the younger was Rachel. ¹⁷ And Leah's eyes were weak, but Rachel was beautiful of form and face. ¹⁸ Now Jacob loved Rachel, so he said, "I will serve you seven years for your younger daughter Rachel." ¹⁹ Laban said, "It is better that I give her to you than to give her to another man; stay with me." ²⁰ So Jacob served seven years for Rachel and they seemed to him but a few days because of his love for her. (Genesis 29: 9-20)

The story is very interesting. When Jacob got to his uncle's city, he waited at the well and saw Rachel coming to make the sheep drink water. He liked Rachel and they both agreed to walk the walk of life together. Jacob spoke to Rachel's father, and the prerequisite was established. The uncle gave his requirement for Jacob to marry his daughter. ***In the spirit realm, do you know the requirement it takes for people in your family to get married? Do you know what is required to make progress in your life?***

Even with Jacob's salary, there were requirements. ***For you to get your promotion, do you have any idea what the spiritual requirement is? Spiritual requirements are the things you must do in order to break out of the family cycle.*** Hannah had to give a double portion prayer for her son Samuel to be born; and she received a double portion offering from Elkannah, a double portion of love, and double portion of many other things. Elkannah said to her, "Am I not worth to you more than 10 sons? (1 Samuel 1:8)" Yet you must engage to confront in prayer and offer the spiritual requirement.

Now Jacob agreed to serve seven years for Rachel, and He dedicated seven years of his life for the woman of his choice. He gave seven years of his life to be with Rachel; this is very important to note. I strongly believe that Jacob accepted seven years, not because it was just a woman, but he also ignored the spiritual implications. All that he wanted was Rachel. *Everything has a price tag on it in the physical realm; the same is true in the spiritual realm.*

It even says in the Bible that it seemed to Jacob like a few days; that's how much the man was willing to push for Rachel. Even when the uncle exchanged the woman he would marry, Jacob chose to give another seven years for the love of his heart. I want to add emphasis here and switch if possible, dear ladies; if a man is not willing to pay the price of sacrifice, believe me, he will not treasure you. However, you may have to pay the price to be with him. The story of Jacob at his uncle's house shows us a great sign of sacrifice for love, exhibited by Jacob. In life those who sacrifice to be with you, in good times and in bad times, are those that truly love you.

A relationship is based on four components:

A. Acknowledgement
B. Consistent behavior
C. Active listening
D. Commitment to the person you love

Jacob worked for whom he loved; I want to change subjects, but something is pulling me to talk about this for a bit. I know we live in a democratic world, and there is what you call gender equality. I get all that, and before you shut me down, hear me please. How is it that, even with all the advancement and all the rights, relationship in our era no longer last? Just look at the escalating number of divorce rates; it is very scary. People no longer value relationship. They are in for their own interest or for what the relationship makes them look like on the outside.

We have less and less people willing to commit to a relationship! Although we have all of this advancement working for us, we have lost touch of the fundamentals. I heard a story that left me wondering and asking questions like how long and how far are we going?

I heard of a man who started asking his wife to pay half of the household expenses – that is, 50%. By the way, if you look at the statistics of why relationships fall apart, you will be amazed to see that money is the number one cause of break-ups in relationships. So, the lady said that she didn't have the money because her job did not pay her enough to be able to pay her husband 50%. As a result, the husband got upset and kicked his wife out of the home. The lady asked, "How is it possible that you want me to pay 50%? How on earth do you want me to respect you?" *You earn respect by being responsible.*

Jacob gave 14 years of his life just to get Rachel. Just because Rachel was pretty special, he desired and wanted her. In life anything beautiful is attractive, and anything one loves, one will want to pursue until it is attained. It was the same scenario with

Jacob; he was very persistent, albeit he was deceived. Laban was a very intelligent beguiler, and he tricked Jacob.

In the spiritual realm, people get their destiny switched with somebody else's, for example, assuming you were the one to get that job, but the forces of resistance switched you with someone else. This is to keep you in the same position so that you end up frustrated. Simply refuse to be switched when it's your time to be promoted and to shine.

In life you cannot have two heads – one must be the head and the other, a partner. In our jobs and enterprises, we have one head that leads and others supporting the head, yet in our homes, we want democracy and equality, which is why people are happy at work yet miserable at home. It just does not work. In the past there was a lot of abuse committed against ladies; however, we must still restructure our homes. Man, take up your position and lead your home – not by being bossy, but lead it by example.

How on earth did Jacob not realize that it was not Rachel! Most of the time it is the demons of our family that follow our bloodline; they often blind us not to see things the way they should be, until we make a mistake that will cost us, and then they leave. I believe Jacob was blinded by the gods that Laban served to keep and maintain the customs of that place. Laban probably chanted Jacob's name all night before he sent Leah to him. Jacob was not aware of what was happening behind the scenes.

Jacob was surely blinded by the principalities that ruled over that place. They made Leah look like Rachel for a while, and after Jacob knew her, her face changed to Leah. I am simply pushing my thoughts beyond the limits here. I once looked at a picture of a young lady – she was so beautiful, but the moment she posted another picture, she looked like an old lady in a younger lady's body. My eyes were opened to see that things were happening in the realm of the spirit.

The Bible says that when Jacob woke up in the morning and realized that it was Leah, he did not even address her, but went straight to Laban and asked him, "What is this you have done to me?" (Genesis 29:25), meaning his uncle tricked him by given him Leah instead of Rachel. *What have you done to me that I committed this big mistake? I acted out of character all night; only in the morning did I come to realize what happened.* Jacob's question, "What have you done to me?" reveals that something was wrong in his dealings with his uncle Laban. People have the capacity to do things against you in this life. People go to places to lock up your destiny and success, but you are more than a conqueror. *What have you done to me? What did you do to me that I spent a night with Leah when I thought she was Rachel? What did you do to me that I was blinded for a while until the end of the issue?*
I once heard a story in which a man said to a lady that all the spirits that he serves will now follow her everywhere she goes on this earth, just because they had an issue. The life of the lady was filled with mysterious things up until now.

In this life, I have seen things that people do that shock me. One time I had a dream in which I saw a lady bossing someone around; I knew the person that the lady was giving orders to very well. The lady was beating her and telling her to work like a slave. When I saw what the lady was doing to her, I got angry in my spirit and asked her if she was ok. She said to me out of fear that yes, she was ok. The funny thing was that when the woman who was beating her saw me, she stopped. These things happen in our lives just like in that dream, yet we do not pay attention to them.

Most of us come from a family that has bondages in certain areas of life, and when that bondage is in manifestation, we are blinded to reality and our purpose. Due to the bondage, at the end, you ask yourself, "Why did I do that?" Here you are feeling so bad after repeating the negative cycle.

Let's go back to the story of Jacob, a very fascinating story if you follow it very carefully. It is the answer from his uncle Laban that says it all: "*It must not be done so in our tradition, to give the younger before the firstborn*" (Genesis 29:26). The traditions in that place decided who got married and when. You could not change it or do anything against it; you had to bow to that tradition. Jacob tried and he was brought to subjection, obligating him to obey the traditions and customs. Do you realize that Laban was his true uncle, I mean, his real uncle from his mother's side?

In other words, if the firstborn has not moved, nobody else will move. If the firstborn does not progress, nobody else will progress. If the firstborn does not succeed, then everybody will be stuck where they are. Unless the firstborn marries, no one can marry. The fact that you are a Christian does not change that. Maybe you will say no, you are too powerful or above that, but it's not true; you have to work to overcome. Jesus did not go to Heaven to enjoy and relax, but He is close to the father interceding on our behalf. Only prayer will help us stand and break out of family and life bondages.

You mean to tell me that if the firstborn is not moving I'll be stuck here? That's right, you heard me well. *Who do you think you are?* What I am stating here is that there are traditions that you *must* overcome. ***Engage to confront!***

There are some customs in our families that must be changed spiritually. If not, we will be stuck under these powers that have been there for generations. These traditions have been set before we even came to earth. Just in case you do not know, every family is ruled by a demon. This demon pursues all the family members throughout life to make sure that they stay within the established boundaries and limitations in the spirit realm. Just as we have border patrol in the physical realm, so it is in the spiritual realm – they patrol the family limitations to make sure that no one carrying your bloodline ever crosses them.

There are families like Laban's family in which there is a spiritual law that *it must not be done so*, regardless of who you are. What Laban was saying to Jacob was this: *you are not going to get what you want here; our customs and traditions determine who deserves it. Also, we have a rule that governs this family, and this rule is that we do not give the younger before we release the firstborn. Our traditions determine what everyone in this family must be.*

Can you imagine that there are families in which there are no older people, since everyone dies young? Thus, refuse to be ruled by the traditions of your father's family and your mother's family in the name of Jesus. There are families in which nobody is stable in life – health wise, financially or academically. How is that possible? Something is not right here.

Let us think for a bit. After Jacob had received all these words of blessing and saw heaven with angels descending and ascending, that did not forbid Laban to put him under the "Labanic" system. Most believers think that simply being a Christian settles everything; who said that? Even Jesus said, "I am the way, the truth and life" (John 14:6). He never said I am the way, that's it; no, it means more work required for the truth and the life.

I heard a preacher once say that Jesus is the door; if you just say he is the door you will die at the door. But He is also the truth and the life. You must press till you get to life, the Zoë life.

I said it earlier, but let me say it again: *your prophecy does not replace your prayer life*. Just because you have received a prophecy does not mean that the devil is afraid of you. You must engage to confront.

Laban said to Jacob, "It must not be done so*," there is a rule here that we put you under*. I don't know for certain but I believe that this Labanic system blinded Jacob all that night to receive and consume what he did not work for.

Jacob worked seven years for Rachel yet at the end Laban gave him Leah. How many of you work so hard and never receive what you work for, only to receive something similar to blind you of your full potential. Why does your family experience what you experience? Is it Coincidental? I do not think so.

Jacob could have been happy with Leah, but he realized, *I offered seven years of service without pay for Rachel, and look at what I am getting today.* You must come to your morning, where you wake up to yourself and find out that you are better than this.

Question: What have you been receiving in this life? Do you receive delays in life or is there an exchange? *It must not be done so in our customs to give the younger one before the older.* The set order had to be respected and followed even if God opened a way for Rachel, the second born, to break out. Just because you have not broken through does not mean that you have wasted your life waiting for what you prayed for; keep pushing forward. May you receive what belongs to you in Jesus' name.

Whatever plateau is in your family, it must not be so. People must be able to go pass through limits and break ancient barriers.

The fact that you are a Christian does not mean that you will escape the customs and traditions of your bloodline or of your family. Traditions and customs are the things that have been established throughout the years and affect people's lives to a degree that you have no idea about. People's lives have been affected by the customs and traditions of the family they come from; it's as simple as that. You may wonder: *I don't know if the reason people in the family live or behave the way they do is because of a pattern in the bloodline.* The worse thing in this life is **to live and be ignorant of what is happening around you**.

You cannot afford to be ignorant of your family's situation and "mode de vie". Allow me to use the French expression in this part; I simply like it. "Mode de vie" means one's lifestyle, or the repetitive things happening in your family. Even medical science believes in what I am talking about. If you ever filled a form from your doctor's office, this is how they paraphrase it: *Did anyone in your family ever suffer from cancer, heart attack, diabetes, etc.?* They want to know the medical history of your family. Life insurance companies are very particular on this; they base their rates on these answers, as they want to know and determine the risk they are undertaking.

Laban told Jacob, *it must not be done so in our customs to give the younger one before the firstborn.* Your bloodline carries something that you must find out about and arise in prayer to have control over it. I was watching TV one day and there was a gentleman who was talking about genetics. He said something that struck me and made me think. He said **every gene carries something**. Wow – I was extremely touched and blown away by that statement. Every gene carries something, whether it is the genetics of a tree or animal; that's why they produce according to their kind.

What the devil has done is blind people with religion; yet go through the family customs and the genetics they carry, even after they speak in tongues and fall under the anointing. The truth is, you must break those family ancient barriers and be free.

I want to conclude this chapter by noting that Jacob woke up in the morning and realized that Leah was not what he had worked for, what he had lived for and what he expected after 7 years of labor. This means Rachel got switched against her will. In the upcoming chapters, I will show you why I am making this claim.

I do not want to close this chapter without taking time to pray.

1. You shall move every barrier placed before you bring delay or exchange in Jesus Name, for Laban said we will not give the younger before the firstborn.

2. Break out of the traditions of your family.

3. Break every limit established in the spiritual realm to restrict your life.

4. Break every code that your genetics carry, which are responsible for any turmoil in your life.

CHAPTER 3
Cancel the Exchange

1 Kings 3:16-28 (NASB) reads as follows:

> *[16] Then two women who were harlots came to the king and stood before him. [17] The one woman said, "Oh, my lord, this woman and I live in the same house; and I gave birth to a child while she was in the house. [18] It happened on the third day after I gave birth, that this woman also gave birth to a child, and we were together. There was no stranger with us in the house, only the two of us in the house. [19] This woman's son died in the night, because she lay on it. [20] So she arose in the middle of the night and took my son from beside me while your maidservant slept, and laid him in her bosom, and laid her dead son in my bosom. [21] When I rose in the morning to nurse my son, behold, he was dead; but when I looked at him carefully in the morning, behold, he was not my son, whom I had borne." [22] Then the other woman said, "No! For the living one is my son, and the dead one is your son." But the first woman said, "No! For the dead one is your son, and the living one is my son." Thus, they spoke before the king.*
>
> *[23] Then the king said, "The one says, 'This is my son who is living, and your son is the dead one'; and the other says, 'No! For your son is the dead one, and my son is the living one.'" [24] The king said, "Get me a sword." So, they brought a sword before the king. [25] The king said, "Divide the living child in two, and give half to the one and half to the other." [26] Then the woman whose child was the living one spoke to the king, for she was deeply stirred over her son and said, "Oh, my lord, give her the living child, and by no means kill him." But the other said, "He shall be neither mine nor yours; divide him!" [27] Then the king said, "Give the first woman the living child, and by no means kill him. She is his*

mother." ²⁸ When all Israel heard of the judgment which the king had handed down, they feared the king, for they saw that the wisdom of God was in him to administer justice.

In the previous Chapters we talked about being switched spiritually, so in this story you will see how the dark world works in switching people up. This story really touched me the first time I read it, and later on, the Lord gave me a revelation that I want to share it with you to whet your appetite for prayer.

Let us look at the following facts:

1. **There were two harlots living in the same house.** I assume that they were friends because not only did they share the same profession, but they were also living together in the same house. Not everyone who lives with you is with you. Let that principle sink into your mind. You must not get fooled by the kindness and smiles of people; often these are just mere ways of manipulation.

2. **They enjoyed the same profession.** They probably met at their place of work and decided to live together, most likely to share the cost of living. Perhaps one lured the other to live together. Be mindful of those you live with; some will trick you to switch your destiny with theirs. Also, be mindful of deception. Ask the Spirit of God to help you know the people you will work with, live with, marry, partner with spiritually, but not only emotional and physical compliments.

3. **They got pregnant almost at the same time.** One thing you have to know about prostitution is that they avoid being sick

and getting pregnant, because it puts their business in jeopardy. How in the world did they both get pregnant almost at the same time? If only one got pregnant I would have understood, but two at the same! This puts a lot of factors in place. It means they had the same menstrual cycle and produced eggs at the same time, and were pregnant at the same moment in their lives. This is too much information to ignore the spiritual connectivity.

4. **They gave birth in the same house,** almost at the same time. I do not think all these facts are coincidental. I do believe that the Holy Spirit had placed these details together for us to find out something about how the satanic and demonic systems work. The Apostle Paul stated that he did not want you to be ignorant of the devil's devices. The dark world work proficiently, why do I say that, they do not reveal plans against your life, yet you always talk about what you want to do in life. Do not be ignorant of the schemes of your enemies; they are willing to do anything that it takes to get their way. People are willing to go to the cemetery to enchant your name, even at late hours, just because they want to hurt you. So, remember things don't just happen.

5. **Both gave birth to boys.** Wow, this is amazing. Why would the Bible give such specific information? I believe it's because the Holy Spirit wants to show us something. Boys carried the family name. I strongly believe that they came to a point that they accepted becoming pregnant, because they were tired of the life they were living and needed hope; so

the sons were the hope of these women, just as the Son of God, Jesus, is the hope for humanity.

6. **They went to sleep almost at the same time;** however, one slept safely and soundly knowing that she had her child close to her, and the other slept carelessly to the point she killed her own son. It is very rare to see a mother sleep on her child, knowing that mothers are very careful when it comes to their children. The story gets interesting here. When they went to sleep, one of them (whose name the Bible didn't mention) slept over her son in the middle of the night and the son died. *If I am really your friend, why didn't you tell me when such a thing occurred? Why do you want to take advantage of me and challenge me to kill my son too?* The heart of man is desperately wicked; the friend that lived together with her, who did everything with her, now wants to betray her love for her friend by sharing unwarranted stories to be believed by the king, so that the baby can be killed. Remember, whatever the plan of the evil one is to switch or destroy your future, God will surely turn it into good.

7. **She slept over her hope and the hope died.** When she realizes that her son was dead, she woke up in the middle of the night, and instead of telling her friend, "My son has died! No! No! No!" she perceived that her friend was sleeping deeply, got in and exchanged the baby.

Let me stop there for a bit. The last time I was preaching at a church, I said something and started laughing by myself. Later on I said, "Please do not wake up in defeat," meaning that if you sleep and dream that someone is beating you up, do not wake up in defeat and panic. If you want to wake up, please tell yourself that there is no way you can wake up being defeated in your dream. You must sleep again, keep that battle in your mind, and fight that devil again until you win, for *it is not over until you win*. People laughed that day, but it is true.

If the harlot had to do an exchange, she could have gone somewhere else or told her friend that she made a mistake, but she did not want to wait another nine months for the full pregnancy cycle. She exchanged her friend's baby for her dead child, a friend who lived in the same house. Because someone is close to you does not mean that he or she wants to see you happy in life. This child represented the future of these women, yet she went ahead and exchanged the baby. We live in an era where people are self-centered; they only think about themselves and are willing to do wickedness just for their own interest.

8. **Let's consider that the two harlots living together at the same place means sharing the same faith, attending the same church and believing in the same Church doctrine.** What I am referring to concerns both people in the Church as well as people out of the Church. Sometimes people in the Church are more wicked and driven by evil than those outside of the Church. I think I will leave it right here, please, for I really do not want to continue on this subject. Most of us that have been in Church for a while can testify that we have found wicked people in the Church.

When I started the ministry I am now in, it was a fellow pastor who told people, "We will give him three months and he will shut down." This was a fellow man of God cursing the work of God – can you imagine? If you do not like me do not say anything. I refused it and broke it, but before that, I want to tell you that every time we grew as a church, after 3 months people would leave the church and we would have to start all over again. That curse word the fellow pastor spoke was in operation until one day I got upset and decided to rise up in prayer to break the curse words hanging over the ministry.

Prior to that it was difficult to experience the presence of God at church, the atmosphere was so dry. So I petitioned heaven; I decreed and declared that *it must not be done so, in the name of Jesus*. You see, what I am saying is that, by the grace of God, we are now on our fifth year of ministry and God is moving us from one dimension to another. Do not let the curse words of your enemies hang over your life. Some of those words you will hear personally, yet others will be reported to you; in either case, you have the key to refuse to be bound by people's words. Do not think that because they are with you in the same house, they want to see you prosper. Big no, brethren.

In this life, you really have to know that everyone that looks at you does not look at you with the same impression that you have. Some look at you because you are beautiful or cute for admiration; some look at you from the mindset of what they can get from you; and some look at you to see what you can deliver for their own interest, so be extra careful.

These two harlots lived together; and just because we are in the same house does not mean we have the same value. If we are in the same church, it doesn't mean we have the same godly character. Furthermore, not all people in the same church see God the same.

Be careful who you call your friend and who lives with you. In the story we are looking at, you would think that knowing the conditions they both were subjected to, the one harlot would have pity and mercy on her friend, but not at all. Again, in this is life people are looking out for their own interest, for what is good for them. Tell me, please, if this act is not witchcraft, nor wickedness in broad day light!

Declare this with me: Whoever is trying to switch my destiny, my hopes and my future, I bind you in the name of Jesus.

The harlot exchanged the child while her friend was in a position of weakness, while she slept. I wonder how many things that belong to you get exchanged in the night season.

A lady came to see me one time in my office and said to me, "Pastor, something is not right in my life." I asked her to please tell me what was going on, and she said, "Pastor, by the grace of God I am quite intelligent, and I have attained a high level of education. I have two Master's degrees and I know I am able to do anything that I want to do in life. Lately, I was speaking to a sister and she said to me that the day before she was going to write her exam – and this exam was something that will move her life to the next dimension – in the night when she slept, she dreamt that someone told her that she was going to fail the exam. In the morning when she wrote the exam, guess what. She failed exactly as she saw in the dream. The night whilst I was sleeping, I dreamt that someone came to me and was arguing with me, and out of anger, told me that I would fail the exam. To my surprise I failed the exam too, by three points only. I was almost there; in our study group, I was the only one who understood and explained to others most of the stuff we had learned." The funny thing this lady told me was that during the exam, all of a sudden, she became confused just for a bit, and that bit costed her exam. She had to go back and start again from ground zero.

These things happen in people's lives. Even as you're reading this book you can remember the type of dreams you've been having lately. You yourself can testify that the devil is trying something funny here.

Another lady came to me and said, "Pastor, last night I had a dream that I was sleeping and dark big man came with a hammer and hit me on my left knee. I screamed in my sleep, and the people who were close to me heard me screaming. When I woke up the next day my left knee was engorged. It was big as if I'd had an accident.

These things happen in front of our very eyes, and most of the time we really do not pay attention to them; we let it be and watch life just happen.

> *So she arose in the middle of the night and took my son from beside me while your maidservant slept, and laid him in her bosom, and laid her dead son in my bosom.*

Wait a minute. Am I reading it exactly as it is?

The exchange happened in the middle of the night and while she was sleeping. Most of our future dreams get stolen in the middle of the night. Most destinies get switched in the middle of the night. She could have accepted it and moved on, but she refused, and decided to look intently. I want you to hear me well, please: most people receive bad luck at night.

The woman took the child from the other woman's side to her bosom without the other knowing that something had been exchanged. Wow. How much of your life gets switched without your knowledge? I do not want to make a transaction in life without my consent.

What else has been switched that you have no idea of? Thank God for the morning; as the Bible says, "Sorrow may last through the night but joy comes in the morning (Psalm 30:5)."

The Bible says that when she arose in the morning and looked at the child intently, she realized that it was not her baby. The life that you live, and everything that happens in that life, is it yours? Recently my spirit just became upset with all that the devil and witchcraft does in our lives. I increased my prayer life significantly. Archbishop Duncan Williams said, "If your enemies enchant your name more than you call on the name of your God, soon they will defeat you." That sentence resonates in my spirit every day, I am telling you, even as I am writing this book.

The fact about mothers is that they sleep, but do not joke with their kids. I once saw something that triggered my attention. A mother was in separate room and there were a number of kids in the next room. When her child was crying, she said, "That is my baby!" I asked her in amazement, "How do you know that's your baby?" She replied to me, "I just know."

There is something about mothers and first-born babies. Because the first baby is the joy of their life, you cannot touch their kid anyhow. This woman slept to the point that the baby who was by her side got taken and was switched from her bosom whilst she was still sleeping; how come?

Why bosom? Because whatever comes from your bosom is yours regardless, and she wanted it to be believed that since the dead child was on her bosom, it was obviously her child. Isn't that what the devil does? The devil is a liar. I thank God for the gifts of the Holy Spirit: the gift of vision, words of knowledge, words of wisdom, and the prophetic gift. They help us to know things at a deeper level than they look physically.

I strongly believe that there are mistakes that people make that come from the pit of hell. People tend to accept such mistakes and believe it is their own doing. I can make a mistake, but I am not a mistake.

When the harlot woke up, she realized that it was not her son; she looked intently and knew that this was not who she carried for nine months and bore. I believe that you can intently look at your life and realize that you carry all the abilities and talent to be where you are in life right. Look at it intently and you will see that you are living your mother's life, your father's life, and something must absolutely change.

Do not accept any exchange; you must demand what is yours. Remember, someone has been planning to switch your life with your grandmother or grandfather's tough situation. Why is it that you are committing the same life mistakes your father committed at the same age? This is not coincidence. It means something is wrong somewhere.

I want to give you a few minutes to have an introspective look at your life and see if there was something switched or exchanged at this stage of your life.

When this woman realized that the dead child was not her son, she went to see the king for the reversal of the situation; she cried out to the king. Her cry to the king was based on what she realized was not hers.

I don't know what, but I know that something of yours was exchanged, whether it is your health, your children, your welfare, your career, your academics, etc. You must refuse an exchange in Jesus' Name. You see, many people think things will change. No, *you* must cause things to change. *You are the key in this equation.*

The reason this woman took the matter to the king was because this child that she bore was everything to her, to her life, to her future and destiny, and her way out of the prostitution. Do not let anybody mess with your life; you must reverse the situation. Take the matter to the King in the morning, at noon and in the evening until the case is reversed. When I moved to Canada, I had problems with my papers, and I remember I was in the country for six years yet my situation was up in the air. I decided to take the matter to the King every morning from 5 a.m. to 7 a.m. before going to work. I seriously and ferociously took it to the King. The matter you bring to the heavenly court will determine how long you will stand there for a verdict.

I stood every day in front of the door of the office of immigration. Well, I selected those hours so that nobody would think that I was mentally challenged. I only had one prayer: *I release my paper. Whoever is sitting on the decision, I command you to release it right now.* Your future depends on what has been exchanged, can you see it? The future of this woman depended on the baby that was exchanged in the nighttime.

Prayer Points

1. I cancel and deny every transaction to exchange my future.

2. I refuse everything that was passed on to me in the night season: sickness, failure and doors that have been shut.
3. I declare that my future is not dead, but alive.

4. I declare that I am somebody, I will be somebody, and I am going somewhere with my life.

CHAPTER 4
Breaking the Pattern of Traditions and Customs

Genesis 29:26:

Laban replied, "It is not our custom here to give the younger daughter in marriage before the older one."

The cycle of traditions within the family of Laban

The sociologist Ashley Crossman said, "A custom is defined as a cultural idea that describes a regular, patterned way of behaving that is considered characteristic of life in a social system." I find it to be so true that our social life is affected by the customs that we practice.

Let's now see the difference between customs and traditions. Today's custom is tomorrow's tradition. Both words can be used as synonyms as they press similar contexts, though both are not same. The explanation of the meaning of custom and tradition looks similar. A custom can be a practice or belief that has been practiced by an individual or a group for a long time. Well, that should not be something that has a history of generations. There can be a workplace custom, an institutional custom or a family custom that we practice or something that our parents told us to do.

When a custom is transferred from generation to generation, it takes the form of tradition. Tradition can be thus explained as a custom that people have been following for a very long time.

I want to go to the text right away to see what happened here between Jacob and Laban.

By saying to Jacob, "It must not be done so in our customs," Laban revealed a spiritual law that governed people who were born in that bloodline. Most of us ignore the blood genes in which we are born to. This is very important to know, because it will help you to stand out and to be strategic in prayer to break them so that they do not overpower and control your life.

I read a book that opened my eyes, and I started seeing life differently. By the way, this was not a Christian book. It was a textbook from a university from the Faculty of Psychiatry and Mental Health. In the textbook[3] the author brought up the belief studies by Mr. Kozier in 1987. To paraphrase, while he was writing about all races and their beliefs and cycles, he mentioned the blacks and stated that black families live together with extended families, and that they are always in large numbers as families. He added that the younger ones in these families sometimes hold odds jobs to supplement the family income, and that they have beliefs that still exist to some extent which include voodoo and witchcraft. This blew my mind to know that these are things that exist in our system and people practice these things.

Let me also note that American Indians have high rate of suicide, and have a homicide rate three times greater than that of any race.

It is eye-opening to see the cycle of traditions and power of genes working. This is because someone said *it must be done so* in this place. The American Indians are less concerned about the future as white people are. I can go on and on, but I want us to realize that

---

[3] Louise Rebraca Shives. *Basic Concepts of Psychiatric – Mental Health Nursing (Second Edition)*. J.B. Philadelphia, PA: Lippincott Company, 1990.

customs and traditions are more powerful than demons; they go from generation to generation. *It must not be done so in our customs that we should give a younger before the older.* Even if the older was not up and ready in life, they would rather keep the younger behind the older one who is slow and not advanced.

As for me, I refuse to be regulated by a throng of people that choose to set the course of our family life, as to who gets what and gets to do what? I know that there are customs that will follow you even if you become a child of God and you are born again.

I heard a story that left me wondering and in awe. A lady came from a family where no woman gets married, so she did her best and got married. Soon after the wedding the husband left for a 'business' and left the young wife pregnant with their first baby boy. The man travelled and never came back; he stayed where he went to and got married there. The young lady gave birth to a handsome baby boy, so cute, and the father never saw the child. Today as I am writing to you, the young lady is single like everyone in her family, single and alone.

You must rise to defend your spiritual life with a fight. If you do not fight, nobody will fight for you. Too many people think if they receive a prophecy, it is settled. It is great but it's not enough. You must warfare and fight until the word declared over you becomes a reality, otherwise it will not be materialized. People just get excited and hear what God has for you; it gives people gratification without really having the impact that you need in this life.

After sometime I began to realize that most people just want others to hear what God has for them. They say in their minds, *keep giving it to me time and again.* People get a prophetic encounter, hear the prophecies, go home and keep things the same. The Bible says that when Jesus was baptized, the heavens opened and there sounded a voice from heaven saying, "This is My beloved Son, in whom I am well pleased (Matthew 3:17)." Remember Jesus did not just keep the prophecy and sleep. He worked with the prophecy and prevailed.

Let's see it now in the case of Rachel:

1. **This custom was designed to restrict Rachel particularly not to move at her pace or speed, but according to the cycle of the customs that regulated the family.**
   Even for someone like you, if Leah is not gone out of your life, you will be stuck behind her. Sometimes in families or places of work, just because you just started does not mean that you should be the last to be lifted. In some places they will push you down just because you are new or have just arrived.

2. **This custom declared to Jacob and Rachel that *you should not be what you want, but what they want you to be. You like each other, so what? As long as Leah is still single you are stuck.***
   I remember when I first came to the city to plant a church, I was opening the door where the meetings were going to be held and a gentleman met me at the door.
   He asked me, "What are you doing here?" I replied that there would be a church in this place starting that coming Sunday. He then asked me who the pastor would be, and I was afraid to say

it was me because I had no experience. I had never pastored a church before. I knew I was coming from being a youth pastor under Dr. Ralph Dartey and that was it; I did not know much about ministry or leading a church. I said to him reluctantly that the pastor would be me. He replied, "Are you going to be able to do it? This city is very hard. I have seen people come in and close down."

I was afraid as I listened to this talk. I became very afraid, even to open the door of the church building, so I asked him, "Sir, what do you do?" He replied, "I am a Bishop. I've had a church in the city for twenty years." Politely, I answered him, "Sir, if you were able to do for twenty years, I do believe that I will be able to do too."

After I said that, he did not say anything, but deep inside of me I knew that my only way to make it in the ministry would be by prayer and fasting. I became a "prayerholic" every day from 5 a.m to 9 a.m. non-stop. I prayed my way into the ministry and the Lord came through for us. In three years we were able to cross the 100 people barrier in a city where most churches are just around 20 to 30 people.

3. **Jacob worked an extra seven years just get where he had to get in life. Jacob was not lazy man but a hardworking man, yet his 14 years were wasted due to this custom.**
   Can you imagine with me for a moment that this man worked seven years twice to get Rachel, whilst he planned to only work for seven years, because of the established customs of the place?

Question: How long is it taking you to be or to do what you want in life?

4. **Jacob faced the resistance from the Labanic system and he was in servitude.**

   When Jacob made the deal with Laban for Rachel, Laban knew that there was a custom in place and that Jacob would not get what he wanted. There was also a servitude spirit in operation, with Laban thinking: *he must serve me and my cause until we are done with him.*

5. **Who are you serving unconsciously?**

   Jacob thought he was serving for Rachel, but in reality, he was serving the system cycle and tradition put in place.

6. **If Rachel never rose up to wrestle, Joseph's star would have been quenched.**

   This I will look at it in the upcoming chapter. It is amazing how parents' prayers affect and influence their children's destiny.

7. **The fact that you carry great prophecy does not mean a thing in the eyes of the witches of your family and the jealous people of this life.**

   Laban never knew what God said about Jacob, but at this time it was no longer Laban working against Jacob, but the customs of the family. The cycle took over his life. I want to you to realize that people should have been serving him according to the prophetic declaration of his father, yet Jacob was serving people under the cycle of the traditions in the family he joined himself to.

8. **Most people are in trouble today, not because they have done wrong, but because they've joined wrong people in their life.** Most people are troubled just because they've knit themselves with wrong association, be extra careful and vigilant those you associate with.

9. **Let me ask you something sincerely; what are the traditions of your family that have been reoccurring from one generation to another?** Can you put a finger on those cycles of customs that do not allow the younger to go before the first? If Laban never opened his mouth, nobody would have known the system and tradition in which that family was governed by. There was a law that governed that family: the younger ones do not go before the firstborns. What law governs your family? I know you are a believer, but can you look into what I am saying?

10. **Every family is governed or regulated by a demonic system. Whether it is witchcraft, voodoo, or sorcery, you must put a finger on it, and deal with it.** Just to let you know, nobody will be able to break through until a person from that family rises up. The funny thing is this: Jesus said in Matthew, 18:18 that: "…whatever you bind on earth will be bound in heaven, and whatever you lose on earth will be loosed in heaven." I want you to hear me very well: if you do not bind, they will bind you. Like today, we have a lot of believers, good people and nice folks, but who are bound and they don't know that they are bound. Going to church does not help you escape the cycle of traditions, but it is your prayers that will help you rise above it to be influential and make an impact

in this life. Too many believers are bound by all kinds of problems and things. They are bound in a life of misery, pressure and are stuck, unable to really make stride and break out in life.

11. **Laban wanted Jacob to be his slave. Can you imagine? Seven years was not enough, but he wanted seven more in order for Jacob to have Rachel.**

The sad part of life is to be a slave and never know it, being used and never knowing that you are being used. Your prophet will not be able to break it; they can help you rise, but you must deal with it yourself. That's why Jacob spent the whole night in order to deal with it. We will get to it in the upcoming chapter. Before I conclude this portion, I want you to take a minute and put a finger on some doings and practices in your home. Family, you must deal with it. They said it must not be done so; you must rise up in your spirit to declare back that it *will* be done so, that everybody in this family can do what they want to do in life and no body or custom will deny them access.

12. **The Labanic system made Jacob receive Leah in the night instead of Rachel. I do not know if he was being blinded, but he received the package without checking it.**

How many of you receive stuff in the night, and in the morning when you wake up, you realize that it was not a dream, but you really received them? Remember the woman I wrote about earlier, who when she slept, saw a man with rod who hit her knee with it, and when she woke up, could not walk anymore. Yes, she was hit in the night whilst sleeping, then in reality felt the magnitude of the pain. You must not take these things lightly; rebuke them and bind them. Personally, I think Jacob should have returned the package the same night, because keeping the package made him take it and consume it.

I refuse to receive things in the night that do not belong to me. Rachel was the expected answer, yet Leah found her way in a place where she was not, and this delayed Jacob for 14 years. Whatever has found its way to you that you never expected to delay you, refuse it. In other words, Leah was used as the delay agent. I refuse to receive Leah answers in the night; Leah was a schemed answer to bind Jacob to never really experience his true life and to keep serving Laban. There are people when you serve them, they will do everything to entice you by schemes and manipulations to keep serving them. But I say they have lied; you will break out of the nest and fly free like a bird.

Prayer Points

1. Overthrow the system that governs your family. Is it a sickness or a sin that walks through generations?
2. Refuse to be bound by anger that runs in your family.

3. Refuse to serve the customs of your family.

4. Declare that you will not be a slave of the cycle of your family traditions and customs.

CHAPTER 5
I Wrestled Against My Sister

Genesis 30:8:
"Then Rachel said, 'I have had a great struggle with my sister, and I have won.' So, she named him Naphtali."

Rachel was the girl that Jacob liked from the beginning. It is very interesting that Rachel got to the point that she wrestled with her sister. There is no place in the Bible that Rachel fought physically, yet she declared when her servant gave birth that she had wrestled against her sister and prevailed.

I want to repeat, there's no place in the Bible where it was written that she got physical with her sister Leah. In Chapter 30 verse 8 the Bible clearly states that Rachel said she *wrestled against her sister and prevailed*. Rachel got duped at her wedding, and now that Jacob paid the dues, she could not conceive. I strongly believe that Rachel realized that she had been programmed in her family to be second in life, never to be first.

There comes a time in life where you cannot take it any longer. *Why? Do you have to take what life hands you?* She wrestled with her sister, the Bible says. I do not think the problem was her sister, but the system in which the sister belonged to. Remember her sister was probably there when the schemes against her life were being constructed. *It must not be done so that we give the younger before the first born.*

Rachel moved Leah out of her way to begin to do things that she could not do. Not only that, she was restricted to be with Jacob, and could not conceive. Remember one thing leads to another.

I am just imaging how that could be. Rachel rehearsed for the wedding, practiced the dance and waited for the big moment of the wedding – the big kiss – that, however, never came. The day of the event she got switched and was replaced with her sister. I can even go further than that. The Pastor blessed her and Jacob for the wedding. When it came time for the honeymoon, she was told something like, "Where do you think you are going? Stay here, you cannot go before your big sister."

Most of the attendees were excited because of the ceremony but they didn't know there was a switch. She got switched – not during the day, but at night. During the day everyone celebrated her and congratulated her, and at night she got switched. Can you imagine waiting to consummate your marriage and being told, "Look here, you cannot go before your sister; it is the custom that your grandfather left in this family and everyone must abide by it. You cannot go." She probably said, "Why daddy? Why daddy?" I can hear Laban say to her, "Look young lady, I do not care if that boy, my nephew, likes you or not. Your big sister must go first. You will have to wait if he's willing to work another seven years for you. If he likes you enough, he will do it; otherwise, wait for the next person that will be interested in you, Rachel. I am so sorry. I cannot break the traditions and customs of this family."

Rachel saw the same man telling her, "Look, I still want you and I'm going to work another seven years just for you." And Jacob worked another seven years to get her; however, she could not conceive. There are roads in life that you must walk alone. People can sacrifice for you to a certain point, yet this road, Rachel had to take and walk alone.

Now Rachel is married to the man Jacob, the man that had a promise that his descendants will be blessed. And she saw Leah give birth four times.

This is what I think Rachel was thinking at this moment:

1. **She thought that things would just change; that is being naive.** I heard someone once say, "Let just give it time, for it will change with time." I laughed because only physical things are affected by time, not spiritual things. Nothing will change if you do not engage in changing them. You must invest your energy in order to break out.

   Rachel made up her mind that she had to wrestle. The stronghold of your home must feel your sweat in order to let go. You've got to labor just as a woman labors in order to bring forth a child. The sad thing is when you carry potential and it never materializes. You are born with potential, but you must become the potential you carry.

2. **Rachel wrestled against her sister because her sister represented the entire household system that pushed her to the bottom in life.** In reality it was not really her sister, but the wicked schemes of her father's house. What is the wickedness of your father's house? What is the shame of your family? If she

never wrestled with everything that was on the inside of her, she would have struggled. She was pushed to the back of the line by a force stronger than her, yet she decided to take it upon herself to fight.

Most believer today think the anointing from the prophet or the man of God will just solve everything without their effort being applied. You need the anointing from the man of God to push you to break out. You see, every family has a wicked thing that nobody comprehends, yet it happens.

3. **The name Naphtali means: "I have prevailed,"** yet the name really meant the place or moment marked for change in her life, where things began to change. You know when at a certain point, you have all things moving smoothly for you, but immediately things begin to shift? You must push back with prayer. In the struggle for success, prayer is not a condition, but a lifestyle.

4. **It was not Rachel who gave birth, but she won because she wrestled.** There is victory that you must experience. While you are reading this book, read until the last page and experience breakthrough. What you are doing is breaking into new ground in the spirit because the upcoming generation will not start from ground zero, but where you have stopped.

5. **The main purpose of wrestling is to maintain your adversary under control where you become superior to them.** Until you raise yourself up spiritually, you will keep getting Leah, spending 14 years of waiting; that is spiritual delay. What it takes others to do in one year, for you it takes years before you

see something coming. This is a new era for your life. You will not be limited where the previous generation of your family has stopped. God is with you. Make your own imprint in this era, spiritually.

6. **Rachel wrestled against the system represented by her sister.** You are probably wrestling against witchcraft, jealousy, hatred and malice. You must prevail over it. You must wrestle until you win, and your spirit will know that this time, you've prevailed.

7. **Mr. Devil, I have allowed you to rob me for a while now and I know how to wrestle;** I shall be relevant in life.

8. **"I wrestled..." When it comes to wrestling, it is your responsibility.** It was her servant who gave birth but she wrestled.

9. **If she could wrestle with her sister than she could have wrestled with witchcraft, spirits and powers that contend with her. Wrestle! Wrestle! Wrestle until you prevail.** I remember when we did not have a child yet, several times my wife lost her pregnancy. Many times, before she would lose the baby, she would dream that a big dark woman would sit on her womb. In the morning she would have stomach pain and lose the pregnancy. When we got to the eighth one, I got tired of it, and decided to wrestle against these spiritual powers until they release my children. Today I stand to testify that we have a great boy and he is now five years old. And can you guess what his name is? His name is Win. That's right; I called him Win, **Win**

Prince. The reason I named him Win is because I won over the powers that fought against my family and me.

10. *I wrestled against my sister and I won.* Wrestle against the system that keeps you out of your position. Sometimes it is witchcraft, sorcery and divination, or even marine spirits that fight your home and everyone that is born there. Life is always about the value you carry. You increase your mental value by going to school, you increase your financial value by working, and you increase your spiritual value by prayer. The more you polish yourself in His presence, the more you increase your spiritual value. The prayer you raise helps you increase your spiritual value.

I heard a story that really touched my life. A lady was referred to me, and as we sat down at the coffee shop, she began to talk and talked for three hours non-stop. I sat there and just listened to her as she poured her heart with deep things. She said to me, "In my family people are barren. All of my sisters are barren and when I got married, I was without a child for three years until I went to see a man of God who prayed for me and my barrenness was broken. However, when my baby girl grew, one day she slept and died. The same way she came is the same way she was gone, and now I am at the starting point again."

"If your enemies mention and cry your name more than you call on the name of your God, then sooner or later, they will overcome you, even if you go to church." These words from Archbishop Duncan Williams of Ghana resounded in my ears as I was listening to her.

Just one point before I conclude this chapter, because I am excited for the next one. The journey is getting exciting. I might be wrong, but check this with me: the Bible says that Rachel was a shepherdess; as for Leah, I searched and didn't find anything about her qualification or anything of any kind mentioned in the Bible about her. You would think that someone who took her father's business at heart would get favor from her dad, but nope, the spirit that restricts your family has no pity.

Let us take time to pray. Would you close this book and take about 15 minutes to pray the following with me please?

1. Cancel every word that has been declared over your family. For Jacob it was said that it must not be done so. What is it for you?
2. Wrestle in the spirit until you win. You will feel it when your spirit wins. There will be a burden that will be lifted.
3. There is a cycle that must break over you. Repetitive things must end.
4. Declare today that it *will* be done so. You must respond to every verbal declaration that is released against you from the pit of hell. I am somebody, I will be somebody, and I am going somewhere with my life.
5. Shout with a sound of victory, because I know that the energy you invest in your prayer will pay off.

CHAPTER 6

Bind the Strongman of your Home

If you do not bind the strongman, the strongman will bind.

Mark 3: 27
"In fact, no one can enter a strong man's house without first tying him up. Then he can plunder the strong man's house."

There is a time to bind demons, but you have to understand that strong men are a different ball game. Actually, this is the person that keeps the house; he keeps the house under his control. Most believers only deal with the curses, and have neglected the strong man of the family.

The job of the strongman is as follows:
1. To confine, restrain, or hold you by physical force or influence of any kind;
2. To restrain from motion, or from customary or natural action, as by friction; and
3. To engage you in battle so that you are put under subjection and remain in closed circle.

His characteristics are:
- The strongman works in the darkness, yet his influence is felt in the physical.
- Your eyes must be opened to see the strongman.

I have a few questions for you today:
- o Why do things happen the way they happen?

o   Why is it that people behave the way they behave?

Realize that a strongman can sit on people and never allow them to see the light in life. I refuse to be under anybody but Jesus Christ. *Can you shout a great Amen!*

How does a strong man gain access to establish a stronghold?
Here are five points to allow you to see:
1. A strong man is fully armed.
2. He has house he owns.
3. He has goods that do not belong to him; he has stolen them from you and your generation.
4. He trusts in his strength.
5. There is someone greater than him and His name is Jesus.

According to Jesus, there is stuff that belongs to you and you are in the strong man's house.
I heard a story that really troubled me I want to share it with you. A man was told by his uncle, "You, you will go nowhere." Just like Laban said to Jacob, "It must not be done so," this was not only going to stop there. If you look at Jacob's children, they had a problem accepting Joseph's elevation announcement.

Let me get back to the story before I forget it. The man that I started telling the story about, he was a Christian and got a visa to travel to United States of America. The moment he landed in the States the photo on the visa changed to the grandmother's. The officer at the immigration office was shocked to see such a thing; they had to return him to his native country.

I heard another story that made me mad. These stories are real people's stories and not just fairy tales. There was a man who was highly educated. He was looking for work and could not find any. Every time he would go to a job interview, they would tell him he got there late, or that the position was taken. So one time, he was talking to his sister and she told him about the things that happened in the family – that they had locked them up from their village. The man was angry so he bought a ticket to go to his village. When he arrived there, he greeted no one, and at midnight, he woke up and dealt with the strongman that held them under subjection. For three days the man stayed there to deal with the strongman. All night he would command the fire to break the circle that kept them circling at one place. On the third day, he told the elder of the village, "If you guys try to repeat whatever you are doing, I'll be back here again."

The strongman has weapons that he uses which are in the form of demons under his command to rob you.

He has people that serve his agenda and their main job is to take stuff from you. Maybe if I tell you this story, you will understand what I am trying to communicate here. One day I was in my office praying, and a lady who owned a little mall came to me. I asked her what was going on. She said to me, "Pastor, you will not believe what just happened to me! I just opened my store and I sell clothes. My first customer was a lady. She was very bizarre. Pastor, you could smell evil from this lady. She entered my store and touched all the shelves where my products were. I tried to confront her, and when she looked at me, her eyes were like blood. Then she said categorically, "I am a witch; let me do my job. If you make another sound, I am telling you, nobody will see you again from today. I will make you disappear right now." The lady kept quiet and watched this woman literally do her voodoo for about five minutes until she left the store. The lady immediately ran to me and explained what had happened. I told her, "Let's pray," and we prayed, but I said to her that, because of this thing, she will need to invest time in prayer. She said to me, "Pastor, I am very busy woman; I do not have time." A few months later, her store closed down and she was completely out of business.

Why am I sharing these stories with you? It is because a strongman must be dealt with aggressively in order to see the light ahead of you. Why is it that you have no joy, no peace? Why do things seem like they are remotely controlled by someone else? It is because he orchestrates things to steal things from you and keeps them. The strongman stole from your father's generation, your grandfather's generation, and now he wants to keep doing the same job with you; no way. The question is: *what did he steal from you so far?*

The strongman has a place, a house. That is an amazing thing to know.
This means there is a place where all his strategies and plan are made. He does not improvise, but he cooks his plans from his headquarter, a place where he monitors your plans and your life.

He thinks he owns the things he steals.
Whatever he gets his hands on, whether families, humans, souls, finances etc., he thinks he owns it all. He enslaves people and wills that they do not excel in life. His power must break over your life in the name of Jesus. Whatever position in this city that belongs to you, I decree and declare that you receive it.

Realize that the Bible calls him a strongman.

Most believers think the devil is a fool – no way. I am not here to try to magnify him, but Mr. Devil takes time to try to get what he wants. Paul says it very well in 2 Corinthians 2:11: "…lest Satan should take advantage of us; for we are not ignorant of his devices." This is too deep a revelation; *do not be ignorant.* That is the first fact of his devices: he uses things to try to get closer to us in order to get what he desires. A device is *a plan, scheme, or trick with a particular aim.* The aim of the devil is to keep you serving Laban all your life, so that you never become what your prophetic word had declared over you. I refuse it in the name of Jesus.

He is a strongman, but people deal with him like a weak man. You must be determined to deal with him. One day a younger pastor came to me and asked, "Pastor, people are not supporting the work of God. I am the only one working, and I want to go tell them." I said to him, "My brother it's not the people, but the devil who does not want to keep the doors of your church open. You must fight until your finances are released. Wrestle every day for the finances of your church."

There are churches in which people love themselves more than they love the Lord and the work of God. If you have a party, they will spend on themselves more than they would spend on the church project.

There are things that God wants you to own this year; no devil will rob you and try to give it to other people that worship him. He offered Jesus to give him the glory if He bowed down to him in Matthews 4:9. Can you imagine? The devil and his cohort are very deceptive; that's why men ought to pray without ceasing in order to be well informed about the devices of the enemy.

There is someone stronger than him.
Jesus is stronger than the strongman, but you must invest time and energy into the fight. The bible says that at the mention of the name Jesus, every knee shall bow and every tongue shall confess that Jesus is Lord (Philippians 2:10-11). We fight *from* victory, not *for* victory. Jesus has publicly disarmed the works of the devil; this is our confidence in Jesus. Take advantage of the victory Christ has won for us. This makes us stronger than the devil. Nobody is stronger than Jesus, period.

Whoever defeats the strongman must be stronger than him. You cannot plunder his good unless you bind him. In other words, you tie him first. You must bind him with all your warfare prayers and your energy in loving the Lord, looking essentially at how the devil took stuff from your grandparents and left them sick and desolated. You must not allow what happened in previous generations to find its way to this generation. You ought to pray, not sleep. You must not only bind him, but also plunder his goods. He took it from previous generations, now is your time to take it all back.

Just before I end this chapter, do you know that this strongman did not start to steal with you, but started from your great-grandfather and moved on to your father? All the generations from your bloodline have been under his power. You are the generation to stop his influence and robbery over your family.

Take a moment and release all that he has been stealing and keeping away from you. To bind means to **disallow** and to lose means to **allow.**

1. I disallow your witchcraft influence over me and my family.
2. I break your power over me and my family.
3. Now I command you to release our joy, career and breakthrough in the name of Jesus.
4. I command you to release my money and promotion.

Now that you have taken this time to pray, let us move on to the next chapter. I am speaking into your life that you will not be the same after you finish reading and practicing the prayers in this book.

CHAPTER 7
Jacob Wrestled for a New Name

Genesis 32:22-32 reads:

²² That night Jacob got up and took his two wives, his two female servants and his eleven sons and crossed the ford of the Jabbok. ²³ After he had sent them across the stream, he sent over all his possessions. **²⁴ So Jacob was left alone, and a man wrestled with him till daybreak. ²⁵ When the man saw that he could not overpower him, he touched the socket of Jacob's hip so that his hip was wrenched as he wrestled with the man.** *²⁶ Then the man said, "Let me go, for it is daybreak." But Jacob replied, "I will not let you go unless you bless me."*

²⁷ The man asked him, "What is your name?" "Jacob," he answered.

²⁸ Then the man said, "Your name will no longer be Jacob, but Israel, because you have struggled with God and with humans and have overcome."

²⁹ Jacob said, "Please tell me your name." But he replied, "Why do you ask my name?" Then he blessed him there. ³⁰ So Jacob called the place Peniel, saying, "It is because I saw God face to face, and yet my life was spared."

³¹ The sun rose above him as he passed Peniel, and he was limping because of his hip. ³² Therefore to this day the Israelites do not eat the tendon attached to the socket of the hip, because the socket of Jacob's hip was touched near the tendon.

The Angel asked Jacob for his name in Genesis 32:27:

The man asked him, "What is your name?" "Jacob," he answered.

I have been pondering on this for a while. *How is it that you came to wrestle against me and now we just spent the night wrestling? And now that you see you cannot overpower me, you ask me what my name is? What name are you really looking for, the name my parents gave me, the name life has given, or the name that people know me as?*

It's not that the angel did not know his name, but there was a problem in that family: they had the wrong name for the blessings they had to have in their lives.

1) The grandfather was called Abram, which means "father," when he was supposed to be Abraham, "Father of many nations."

2) His father was called Isaac, which means "laughter," because the grandfather laughed when the Angel of the Lord gave him a prophetic message about his birth.

As I just pointed out Isaac means "laughter"; what a name. Now let's look at Jacob. He was called "trickster," "thief," and "manipulator," yet God had placed a blessing on him.

I am so excited to share this. I know it is not part of the message, but I want to share it for it to be blessing to someone reading this book.

In the book of Joshua chapter 2, when Joshua sent the two spies to Jericho to spy on the city, they were accommodated at the house of a prostitute. How is it possible to go on a mission where God has sent you and choose to live with a prostitute? This is not what I want to share, but here is what God showed me: Rahab the prostitute said to the spies that she knew that the Lord had given them the land and their terror had got into her people. I am paraphrasing. So when Joshua and the people got into the land, Joshua told the spies to go to the prostitute's house and bring the woman.

The fortune of the woman arrived, because she helped God's people. Every prostitute's house has a woman hidden in it; you just have to know how to bring her out. The point is that her fortune arrived, and she and her household were spared. Remember, the woman had a wrong name, yet God had a plan for her. Don't just focus on the wrong name, wrong experiences and wrong occurrences. When God comes into the scene, He will turn things around for your good.

Let me get into the idea of having a wrong name, but carrying a blessing. There are people that you see today, they carry the blessing of the family yet the wrong name. I remember my own brother did not like the school system because they gave him a name, just because he had not met their standard. I used to ask myself questions about this, but we did not kill his destiny in that particular moment. Today I am telling you, he is so blessed, with his own business and employees. He carries the family in such an incredible way. I am so grateful to have him as a brother; he is so nice and kind hearted.

What name do you carry in the spirit realm which is part of the Labanic system of your family, that even though you are a believer, they still have a grip on you, manipulating circumstances, appearing in your dreams and violating your territory?

The story of Jacob in the Bible is quite remarkable. He was the man who started wrongly yet moved on well to change the course of his life with a wrestling prayer. I cannot say it enough; I have to repeat it. There is prayer and there is *wrestling* prayer. If it were not so then why did Jesus, when talking to His disciples in Mark 9:28, mention to them that this kind can only go out by fasting and prayer? If I was a disciple that day, I would have asked, "What type of prayer are you talking about, Jesus?"

***I will not let you go until you bless me;* I am not a believer to fill some religious statistic.**

The reason that I am a believer is because I want the Lord Jesus to rule over my life. I am tired of the god in my family to rule over me. We need to have Jacob's determined attitude which was exhibited when he wrestled with the Angel of God. The attitude that says: "I will not let you go until you bless me." Most people go to their church for religious reasons. I do not have time for that. Church becomes church when God impacts your life. Most people attend church because it sounds good, and there are lights and a lot of people. However, are you being impacted? Do you only attend church or do you attend to experience His presence in your life?

What Jacob was looking for here was the blessing that was possible in the spiritual realm, and he wanted to make it possible in the physical realm.

I am determined to make it in this life, because I understand that only God can cause me to break out of the system I am born to. I have seen my uncles struggle, and my mother's sisters really struggle in life. Now when it comes to my generation, I am in charge either to let it happen or to stop it.

I remember a story that happened to my family one time. My mother's sister's daughter passed away and the husband of this aunt got upset and said to my mom, "I will go everywhere to make sure that one of your children also dies." My mom called me, a little worried, and I said to her, "You do not have to worry about a thing." I took the battle in my hands for few nights, and I wrestled against those declarations. Then one day I received a phone call from my mom saying she almost died, and I answered, "How mum?" She said, "There was a car that lost its breaks and it was coming straight in my direction. Everyone ran away and I did not have a place to run to. The car hit me and I fell to the ground. Everyone thought I was dead, but thank God, I stood up and nothing was broken in my body. Praise God!"

There are a lot of declarations that have been made against you or your family, and you must wrestle.
I will not let you go until you bless me. Men can bless you, but your name will still be the same. Although Isaac blessed Jacob. Jacob understood that the next stage in his life was to struggle to breakthrough. Joseph needed to be sold, so that he would struggle to bring out the blessings of the family. Joseph shifted the course of the family pattern. You can also shift the course of your family pattern. Say: *Lord bless me.*

Why was it so important to Jacob to demand a blessing even to a point of a fight?

The Bible says in Proverbs 10:22 that it is the blessing of God that makes one rich and it adds no sorrows to it. It is only the blessing of the Lord that helps to break the limits set by the Labanic system of your family. It's through the blessing that you break out from the system in your traditions that restrict people and confine them to a customized way of living. Jacob saw his blessings and he was willing to fight for them. Do you have an idea of what yours are? If no, start fighting; if yes, continue fighting.

The Angel said to him, "Jacob, let me go for the day breaks." In other words, whenever a day breaks something must change in your life. A day is breaking into a new day, but you keep staying in the old you; how is that possible?

This business of breaking out of the traditions is never done in public. Too many people think just one day of deliverance meeting is all that they need. That isn't so. In order for one to break out of the Labanic system in their family or circumstances, they must keep pressing until something breaks. You Pray Until Something Happens (PUSH)!

How can I let you go when I don't know when I'm going to see you again? Let me tell you, even today's message will never be preached the same tomorrow. Today the Holy Spirit has designed it just for you to receive from today. So, Jacob was right in wrestling with the Angel before he received his blessings.

Story: I was preaching somewhere and there was a lady who said, "I will not go home the same," and she didn't go home the same she came. A year after she had a baby because she was determined to have a breakthrough the same day.

What is your name?

This is not a name everyone calls you, but a repetitive circumstance that keeps happening to you which you have not paid close attention to. Laban said to Jacob, "It must not be done so in our customs to give the younger before the first born." If you look into it very, very carefully, you will discover that it all started from the grandfather, Ishmael. Ishmael was the first born, Isaac was the second born. Now Isaac had kids and the second born got his way to be called the first. It was Laban who revealed the secret of the family traditions when Jacob came to inquire.

Realize one thing: in the case of Abraham and Isaac, the impact was not going to be great, because they both only had two kids. Jacob had 12 children; now imagine the eleventh child trying to tell all his brothers that he would govern all of them. It's something else when only one person hates you, but to have 10 people hating you, oh boy. It's great trouble.

At this time, I can imagine that the night was long when Jacob asked for a blessing and the Angel asked him for his name. *Man, what are you talking about? I want a blessing and you are asking me my name? I just spent the whole night with you and you do not know my name?*

The name the Angel was asking for here concerned his character; *what is the true you*? The true you comes from the bloodline of your family.

Here he said to the angel that his name was Jacob; he did not hide his name. In time past, I was living like Jacob, nothing more nothing less. I was stuck in the Labanic system that took me 21 years to come out of.

What is your name? Your name is not what we use to call you, but what happens to you year in and year out.

Your name shall no longer be Jacob.

I feel like shouting at this part, Amen! Whatever the system has made your name to be, you shall no longer be called by that anymore. The Angel was saying that what people have called you shall be broken today. *You will have a different name, for life respond to names.* Everything functions according to its name, so today you will function and be regarded as prince or princess of God. The last time I checked in the Bible they used to call Hannah and Sarah barren, but the Lord God changed their names when the angel appeared to them with new names. I don't know the names people mock you with at your workplace, in your family, in your vicinity, at school, etc. I am here to tell you that your time has come; your good news from the Lord is here. His message to you is that he makes all things beautiful in His time and that He changes names, just as He did in the Bible. He also brought laughter and joy. Behold, He makes all things new.

I decree and declare that life will respond to you differently because of your new name.

I feel like telling someone that you shall no longer be called sick, poor, broke and unstable. Your name will no longer be as it used to be. People can do whatever pleases them, but the story has changed. This is a new season, a new era, and the new you is breaking out today. You shall be called by a new name. In this season of your life, new openings and new things will happen to you.

Continuing on the Labanic system, the system thought it could restrain and constrain Jacob and his children, but I do believe when Jacob wrestled, he had a prophetic opening in his spirit. He wrestled until that plan was broken over him. Now Joseph could also have said, "You meant it for evil, but the Lord has changed it for good so that I can stand before you today."

For Jacob to pray to God all night, in wrestling prayer, it tells me that if you really mean business with God, something will change over your life. Nothing will help you but your persistence in prayer to God. I heard a man of God say, **"Persistence breaks resistance."** For whatever is possible in the spirit realm will be impossible in the physical realm. Here is what we will do right now; put this book down and do this:

> **I want you to call yourself seven names that you believe deep down in your soul must be so**. Your name is not what others call you, but a name that your spirit testifies that you are.

He blessed him there.

Today is the day of your blessing. Now is the time and the hour to receive your blessings. There is a place for your blessings, and this place is found in prayer. Once you increase your prayer life something will change. The Bible says in the book of James 5:16 that **"the effective fervent prayer of a righteous man avails much."** I once had a dream and saw myself with an Angel of the

Lord. He said to me, "I know you pray, but that is not enough. Can you raise your prayer time to five hours a day? I said to him, "Yes, I will." Immediately at that moment he blew on my face the power of God, which signifies strength. When it hit me, I began crying. I woke up from the dream and saw tears on my face. By the grace of God, I can tell you that from that day, my prayer life has been transformed. Beloved in Christ, I now not only enjoy prayer, but I see the ramifications of my prayer life. I humbly urge you to raise your prayer life.

When prayer goes up, the glory of God comes down. The Angel of God carrying Jacob's blessing of a new name had no option than to bless him before he left, because he saw his determination and eagerness to break out of the system that pushed him down in life. God looks at your determination in order to release something over your life. You must be blessed here, now, *today*. May today be a remarkable day in your life, one in which God has changed things in your life and has made them new.

The sun rose over him because there was a new blessing over him. The sun rose because he had been in the night season all of his life.
Most people walking around, when you ask them the time, they will confidently tell you it is twelve noon. The clock always ticks, every time, but it does not mean it is the time of your life. You must wrestle to cause the sun to rise over you. The night days must end over your life.

> ➤ I decree and declare that the sun is rising up on you and your family.

➤ I decree and declare that you shall no longer be in darkness. Let there be light over your life, finances, career and ministry.

A lot of things begin to change if you stop just praying and invest your energy and sweat into wrestling warfare. I am telling you that even the sun will rise upon you. Nature will begin to obey to your every move.

I cannot end this chapter without giving you an opportunity to renew your passion for prayer. Dear beloved, today our church is more advanced than our grandparents' churches; the church is full of gadgets and lights, yet people in it are empty. You know why? There is a lack of prayer in the house.

I remember when it was 2017 going on 2018, I was praying and telling God that I was tired of just being a preacher, that I wanted to make an impact in this life. He showed me in a dream that I had to preach on prayer. Let me say this to you, my beloved – my life was changed, the level of revelation of the word has increased in my ministry, and the power level has gone up, just like a person going to the filling station to get gas for their car.

Let us renew our commitment for prayer.

Say after me: *Lord Jesus, teach me how to pray, not religiously but by revelation, in the name of Jesus I pray. Amen.*

That's it. My beloved, now find a church that prays and join them – not those who have prayer program, but who have a prayer life.

There is time to pray alone and there is time to join prayer group and get your payer life in motion.

CHAPTER 8
Open the Gate that Leads to the City

Acts 12: 5-10:

> *⁵ Peter was therefore kept in prison, but constant prayer was offered to God for him by the church. ⁶ And when Herod was about to bring him out, that night Peter was sleeping, bound with two chains between two soldiers; and the guards before the door were keeping the prison. ⁷ Now behold, an angel of the Lord stood by him, and a light shone in the prison; and he struck Peter on the side and raised him up, saying, "Arise quickly!" And his chains fell off his hands. ⁸ Then the angel said to him, "Gird yourself and tie on your sandals"; and so, he did. And he said to him, "Put on your garment and follow me." ⁹ So he went out and followed him, and did not know that what was done by the angel was real, but thought he was seeing a vision. ¹⁰ When they were past the first and the second guard posts, they came to the iron gate that leads to the city, which opened to them of its own accord; and they went out and went down one street, and immediately the angel departed from him.*

The story in the book of the Acts of the Apostles is quite remarkable! Jesus had just left the disciples, and now they began to implement the heavenly mandate on earth. At the same time, they were also trying to live the life that our Lord, Jesus Christ lived on earth. **Remember, living a Christian life is different from living the life of Jesus Christ; the Christian life is led by the Spirit of God.** The Holy Scriptures make us understand that those who are led by the spirit of God are the sons of God. When the people in Antioch saw the disciples, they saw Christ in them. When Peter was kept in prison everything was locked down because someone decided to put him in jail to please the Jews.

Similar situations like these are still going on in the world we live in today. There are people in this world that put others in jail and the worse part of life is to be put in jail and never know that you are in prison. As they are physically imprisoned, they are also spiritually imprisoned, whereas someone has the key and locks you down until they decide to undo it.

The following are the key Rhema words we would be considering in the book of Acts, chapter 12:

1. **Peter was kept in jail and the church rose up in prayer.**
   I would like you to pay much attention to this point raised. When Paul and Silas were arrested, they prayed for themselves and heaven responded in a massive way. There was an earthquake, the foundations of the prison quivered and the chains loosened. The Bible stressed that at the midnight, they were praying. As a child of God, what would you be found doing in the midnight of your dilemma? Would it be prayer or complaining? Midnight is a time where a believer is to intercede and not whine about their problems. A songwriter said, "Prayer is the key and it is the master's key." In Relating this story to today's real-life situation, Paul and Silas got arrested by simple men, so they prayed for themselves and they got out of the situation. However, when Peter was arrested, it was by the King Herod, so the impact is was the same. Now you see why the church rose to pray for Peter. Most people are bound by a king yet they try to pray by themselves and nothing happens. The church understood the

essence of joint prayer. They realized they needed to rise up there and pray, for what had arrested Peter was bigger than him, and they had to join forces.

2. An Angel appeared in jail.

The amazing thing was that an angel appeared right in the jail where Peter was kept; that angel was an angel of that church.

Many church angels are currently dusty because the church does not give them missions on earth to bring about great deliverance. In Acts 12, the church stood up and heaven responded. I wonder what would happen in our communities and families if we stopped showing off in churches and really gave ourselves to prayer. An angel of God who was in the corridors of eternity was summoned.

3. Arise, the Angel told him.

In the jail the Angel said to him, "Arise; I am not here to carry you, but to cause you to arise. Arise and defile what has been said about you." Here the Angel of God said to Peter to arise and put on his garment. Though it was dark, Peter rose immediately. We must also arise from our sleep and do the necessary. The reason why you must arise is that people have been praying and interceding for you. Don't you ever think that you are arising in your situation by yourself; what you don't know is that there is an entire praying church army behind you that is carrying you.

4. They passed the first and the second guard.

Although the Angel was there, Peter still had to pass the first and second guard post. Usually when you are a prayer warrior you will notice from your spirit when you have passed the guard post. You must be able to pass those two guards. Although the angel was there, Peter had to pass the guard post that stood in front of him. Those two guards were placed there to make sure Peter was kept in jail no matter what. Now the church understood that if Herod arrests you, you will need the whole body to rise up against him. No guard can keep you behind the line, but you shall break out to shine forth in this life.

5. **They got to the iron gate that leads to the city.**

   Why is the Bible so specific about the iron gates? The writer of the book of Acts made sure that we understood the materials used to construct the gates. The Bible refers to an iron gate that led to the city. This specifies that that city was protected by an iron gate. I discovered from most of the ancient history that cities were protected by walls and gates to prevent intruders from entering the city. I get that, but here I do not think it was just for that. The Bible wants to tell us something that, the city was protected by an iron gate, so therefore anyone who wanted to become somebody had to pass through that iron gate.

   As I was meditating on this scripture, I realized that when Peter passed through the iron gates, all of a sudden they heard a knock on the door at the house where they stayed to pray for him. Immediately, they said it was his angel. Why that statement? It's because he saw the iron gate opened and his own life was opened to the point that his angelic counterpart came out. If you really pay attention to this scripture, you will see that the Bible says the gate opened to them on its own. Does the Bible mean to tell us that gates make decisions? This was not just a gate, it had to open because after it was opened, the shadow of Peter began to heal people. His life was no longer the same when the iron gate opened. You must command the iron gates to open up for you and your family. If there was an iron gate then there must also be a blood gate, an enchantment gate, or evil gate. Isaiah 45:2 refers to an iron and brass gate that was broken into pieces by the Lord. King David said in Psalms 24:9: "Lift up your heads, O you gates! Lift up, you everlasting doors! And the King of glory shall come in."

You want to tell me that, the whole king of glory could not come in because the gate did not lift yet. *Ah yayaya*, in the name of Jesus, may every gate of iron standing before you be broken.

Take a prayer break. Close this book and deal with the gates. These gates must lift up so that the king of glory can come in. After He has come in, you will radiate the Lord's glory. Remember they got to the gates that led to the city; so shall you get there. **Make sure you get there today!**

Prisons don't break by a one-day prayer; it requires consistent prayer. This breaks prison doors. The devil is in his business to put people's destinies, treasures, lives and resources in jail. But I heard in Isaiah 45 the voice of God saying that He breaks into pieces the gates of brass and iron. He gives to his children treasures in darkness and riches in the secret places. He is the way, the truth and the life (John 14:6).

Types of Prisons one could found themselves in:
- ➢ **There are physical prisons**
- ➢ **There are spiritual prisons**

This is when you have broken the established law that is in place; the system places you in prison to spend time there. Also, I must say that some of the people who are in prison are in there for life and some sometimes.

About prisons:

- A lawyer will help you in physical prison. He will plead your case to the judge even if your sentence was going to be longer. A lawyer will reduce your sentence and tell you that you will only spend a couple of months and you will be free. What we do not realize is that being incarcerated could stop the movement of your life. That is the physical thing we observe when we see prisoners. They do not have the freedom to move or improve themselves.
- Just as physical prison stops the movement of your life, so it is with spiritual prison.
- Some people are imprisoned by association; Jacob had a lot of promises of greatness, but his relationship with Rachel brought him under the household god of that family.

Who you associate yourself with can put you under their household god, so be careful!

- In order to get out of prison you will need prayer and the word of God; just as a lawyer will plead and quote the law, so you will need prayer and the word to get out.
- How do you get to jail? It is simply by a word, the pronunciation of a sentence, a declaration by a person who has the authority to do so. It is similar with spiritual things. There are people who are trying to put you in jail, so you must break it with your words. You must respond to every verbal attack with your

words. OUR Lord Jesus Christ overcame Satan in Matthew 4 with the word of God, saying, "It is written…" There is power in your tongue, for God has touched your lips with coals of fire. So whatever you declare and decree shall be established.

- **The prayer of the church will help release you from Herod's prison.** The church knew at that moment that they had to take the matter into their own hands. One thing every believer needs to know is that we should not wait for problems to conquer us. Instead, we need to arise in prayer to overcome the problems, because scripture says that we are more than conquerors. Although Herod is powerful, we have a God who is more powerful than Herod the king.

Before concluding this chapter, I would like to talk about something very important. If you read our main scripture in Acts 12, you will see that the Bible clearly states that **"when they came to the gate that leads to the city, it opened to them out of its own accord."**

Gates that lead to the city:

If this is true for this city, then there are a lot of gates that stand in front of you that must open to you out of its own accord also. Gate here refers to the door of the womb where things are made up and where things comes forth, gates that releases something that you have never had before.

Peter was never referred to as an angel before the opening of the gate that leads to the city; this means that the city was opened to him. I wonder why the people told Rhoda that it was his angel, because the gate of the city was opened to him and his ministry.

Facts about Gates:

1. **A gate always leads to something**

   They do not place a gate for nothing. Gates are placed to lead to something greater and wonderful. If a gate opens for you, it must lead you to something significant in your life.

2. **Gates are placed to protect something**

   They protect houses, compounds and palaces. A gate is there to restrict certain people from having access to your property or treasures. It is there to protect the access way to whatever is behind the gates.

3. **A gate is place to signify the beginning of something**

   This means the beginning of a house, the beginning of a place, the beginning of your influence. A Biblical example is when our Lord Jesus Christ said that He stands at the door and knocks, and if anyone will hear His voice and open the door for Him, He will come in and dine with him (Revelation 3:20). Thus, He is the door that gives a new beginning to whoever welcomes Him in their heart. So, a gate is a place to signify the beginning of something.

4. **Gates mean the end of something**

   You are at the end of something and moving on to the new phase of your life.

5. **Passing a gate means you are entering into someone else's property**

   In this case Peter was entering into a new stage of his life, a new phase of his life. Remember Rhoda said she had seen an angel! Angels bring new things to your life. When are you going to enter into the new phase of your life? Life works in phases, and stages. Be ready, be prepared to allow God walk you through your phases of life. *It's time to arise and pass through your gate!*

6. **When they got there it opened on its own accord**

   It is about time that things begin to obey your stages and your phases of life. Peter was free and the gate opened out of its own accord. The Bible states it clearly that **"when they got there…"** This tells us about time. "When" has to do with time. I don't believe that if Peter was in his jail cell and declared that the gate open up, it would have opened. I really do not think it would have opened. But it opened when he arose and they got there. This is to make us understand that you must gather all your strength in life to get there. Remember, Isaiah 60:1 (KJV) says, *"Arise, shine for thy light is come, and the glory of God is risen upon thee…"* When are you going to get to where your new phase will be? They said it was his angel, and I noticed that Peter entered a new phase of his life. You just have to rise up and do what is necessary.

   When they got there: for Peter, it was his presence. He had to get there physically. However, for you it is your prayer. Your prayer will get you there. Unfortunately, many people leave their prayers in the hands of others. That is why most people tell other men of God to fast for them instead of fasting and praying for themselves. That is why the Apostles said to the congregation, when they had an argument, choose among you men that will serve you. They said of themselves, "but we will give ourselves continually to prayer and to the ministry of the word (Acts 6:4)." Leaders, church members, to whom have you given your prayer life to? Is it to the pastors, prophets or bishops? Your prayer will not be in the hands of intercessors, give yourself to prayer. The last time I checked in the Bible I saw Jesus asking the disciples why they slept during the time they were supposed to be praying (Matthew 26:40). He, the Lord Jesus Christ, was praying during that time. Jesus stressed that they could not even watch and pray for an hour. Beloved in Christ, God does not want us to be lazy Christians. We need to pray! Remember, there are gates in the city that must open on their own accord. *For your prayer is the key to the gates of the city.*

7. A gate brought Peter to the angelic dimension

It was a gate that brought Peter to the angelic dimension because when he knocked at the door where prayer was being lifted up for him, they said it was his angel. At first, Peter was referred to as angel, but when they passed the gates that led to the city, it was something else. Yes, because he crossed a gate of iron which opened up for him, he radiated the Lord's glory and was seen as an angel. You shall also arise with speed in your life. You shall radiate His glory.

A. *I am writing this book for you so you can arise and cross the iron limitations placed in front of you.*

B. *I am here to let you know how to enter into another phase of your life.*

C. *If they used the gate of iron at that time, then it is also possible that you have gates of the blood of Jesus Christ.*

D. *The material used to construct the gate is not your problem; your persistence will break the resistance. Amen!*

CHAPTER 9
Rachel Sat on the Household Gods

Genesis 31:30-34 (NIV):

> *30 Now you have gone off because you longed to return to your father's household. But why did you steal my gods?"*
> *31 Jacob answered Laban, "I was afraid, because I thought you would take your daughters away from me by force. 32 But if you find anyone who has your gods, that person shall not live. In the presence of our relatives, see for yourself whether there is anything of yours here with me; and if so, take it." Now Jacob did not know that Rachel had stolen the gods.*
> *33 So Laban went into Jacob's tent and into Leah's tent and into the tent of the two female servants, but he found nothing. After he came out of Leah's tent, he entered Rachel's tent. 34 Now Rachel had taken the household gods and put them inside her camel's saddle and was sitting on them. Laban searched through everything in the tent but found nothing. 35 And she said to her father, "Let not my lord be angry that I cannot rise before you, for the way of women is upon me." So, he searched but did not find the household gods.*

I am really excited to get to this point. When I started writing this book, I truly never thought my mind could get here and share what I am about to share with you now. It's like God shot a light on me to see something that I have never seen before from His word. No wonder the word of God says His word is active and at the entrance of His word brings enlightenment (Psalms 119:130). I am grateful to God for His grace to cause me to see more from His word.

Rachel, who is now the focal point of this chapter, is the one whom the traditions of the family tried to bury.

When Jacob left Laban, he just wanted to get away from someone who tricks and uses people. Rachel had taken the households god. This is quite fascinating to me because the same household god pushed her behind Leah just because Leah was the first born. Laban said to Jacob on that day that it must not be done so in their customs to give the younger's hand in marriage before the first. If this was true for this instance, then it was true for other things too. It must not be done so to let the younger succeed before the first, to shine before the first. Your physical position in life must not and cannot determine your spiritual position. I find it very difficult to comprehend that Rachel stealing the household god would be something beneficial to her. This household god was in charge of setting customs and traditions, just as it is for your home and my home too. I believe that the Holy Spirit took this part of the scripture and inserted it there to bring light unto us, for us to understand certain truths about these customs. Laban had a god that ruled his home, and that god was in charge of setting rules and regulations of how people should live. For example, in this family of Jacob's, all the women that they really loved could not give birth. Sarah was barren, Rebekah had a problem during her pregnancy, and Rachel had a conception problem too.

Now Rachel took the household god and ran with it.
I don't think she did this to help her in life where she was going. If so then maybe at least her children were advantaged over Leah's children. She took the household god from her father because she did not want her father's house to be ruled by anything any longer; this household god robbed her from her joy in life. The funny thing is this Laban did not press Jacob that much for his girls and grandchildren, but for his god. Laban searched everywhere for his

god; this means this god was very important to him. It was called in the scriptures the household god, meaning the god of the family, the good luck of the family, the family charm.

Let us look at this scenario I had.

One day a young girl called me one time and said to me, "Pastor, I feel like committing suicide right now. My nights are filled with nightmares that you have no idea of. I am troubled and don't know what to do." She added, "My grandma could not give birth and she went to see a fetish man called Marabou. The man took her to a river and there came a being who spoke with the man. After the conversation, the man told my grandma that she would have only girls, but that there would be a problem with the first born. My grandma's first daughter committed suicide, my mother's other sister's first daughter also committed suicide; both threw themselves in the river. Pastor, I feel like I want to die. I am the first born of my mother. I have everything, but I want to die. I feel like throwing myself over the bridge often." This was somebody's life being threatened in front of my very eyes. To resolve the problem I invited the girl to one of our retreats called the Encounter weekend. At this Encounter, she received her deliverance and by God's grace she is now free – praise God!

Rachel took the god of his father's house and ran with it; I do not believe that it was done to keep as a good luck charm or protection of any kind. This was beyond just an image that Rachel took and this was beyond Rachel just stealing things from his father. This was prophetically to make a statement that since she had prevailed against her sister, she wanted to also prevail against the household god. The father came out to look for his god. I wonder why he was so eager about this image that Rachel took. I strongly believe that this god made Rachel's life miserable, so she probably made up her mind that on the day she would be leaving her father's house, she would deal with her father's god. You see, Rachel did not want to see what happened in her generation to ever happen again.

Let us look at some of the characters Rachel exhibited:

1. **Rachel took the household god and ran with it.**

   Why steal the household god? This is to signify that anyone that will be born in this household will not be under the influence and manipulation of this household god. Leah never thought of anything like that, but Rachel did. Sometimes people like things the way they are. You will meet people that want to let things just be the way they are; namely the Labanic descendants. They will fight you not to change anything. Some time ago, I was transferred to a church when I used to work for an organization in the city. I decided to just go for it. When I got there, you won't believe that the leaders of the church prevented me from expanding and growing the church due to some of their church customs and traditions. So, once, when I was deep in the spirit, I found that this must not be done so. Honestly, they fought me until I left that place. Leah never thought of it, but Rachel did! On the day she got switched in the night just before the honeymoon, I believe she got upset and decided to fight the system that was made to restrain her. Here I can boldly say that you must rise up and fight against every evil tradition and household god that brings limitation, retrogression, barrenness, sickness, shame, disappointment, divorce, failure, etc. in all areas of your life. As a child of God, you can do this by your actions, meaning acting with the word of God and through prayer.

2. **Rachel took the household god and sat on it.**

Wow! I know this was to hide it from her father, but was this the only place she could hide this god? Why wouldn't she find another place for it? I was wondering what this could be, but remember in Genesis 30:8 where it says that she wrestled against her sister and prevailed? I do believe that sitting on this god was a prophetic gesture to send the message: *you who sat on our lives, today I will sit on you.* To sit is a position of authority, a position of command, to never ever allow that power to overcome your life anymore. She sat on it prayerfully. You must sit on the god of your family! How do you know that you have a god in your family? When there is a particular thing that rules your home.

3. **You must sit on the god that rules your household.**

You might say you go to church and speak in tongues, that you even have men of God as friends who even remember you in their prayers. Yes, that's good, but it does not make you the exempt from being ruled by the household god. There is a household god that has been in your family for generations, and now you think a small amount of anointing oil you got from prophet will chase it away? I don't know who will make the household god disappear just like that! Stop kidding yourself. The household god in Laban family was not afraid of all the spiritual experiences Jacob had with God. A repetitive or reoccurring thing that happens from previous generations indicates that there is the presence of a household god. *You must be willing to have a fight with the household god and put him under your control.* The witchcraft of your household must know that you are not like the previous generation. Not only are you going to church, but you understand that it will take a fight to break out of that household god. As I was just reflecting, it came to my mind that Rachel wanted this household god to be far from her father's house. You can be out of the household, but not far from the household gods.

4. **It does not make sense for you to leave the house and to take the household god with you.**

   She left with the household god because she was so tired of being a victim of the system established without her approval. If she did not do what she did, the household god would have followed her everywhere throughout her life. In the spiritual realm there is no distance at all, you must deal with it until its breaks.

5. **You might not agree with everything, yet it wouldn't change a thing.**

   Why would I take the household god that has not given me anything in life? Because of democracy, people think they can also argue with spiritual things. The world does not function by democracy, especially the spiritual world. You just have to take responsibility and fight with the forces that want to restrict your family and your children.

6. **Until you sit on it, it will continue to rule over the household.**

Rachel sat on the household god so that her father would not find it and restore the commitment to this household god. She sat on the household god to rule over the power that it had over the family. Although the father was looking for the object, sitting on it tells us that she rules over it now. Therefore, poverty and any other evil thing in your household must be sat on.

7. **For the way of women is upon me.**

She said to her father that the way of women was upon her. What do you mean by that, Rachel? The way of women was just to explain the fact that she was in her menstrual period. When a woman is in her cycle, she has a flow of blood on her. Amazing! What Rachel was saying is that the flow of blood was upon her. She was connecting the future generation to the manner of the cross. Just as the father could not touch her, because of the blood, so it will be with the blood of Jesus on you. John the Apostle said that you overcome by the blood and the word of your testimony (Revelation 12:11). *For the manner of women is upon me*; how coincidental is that to have the manner of women and sitting on the household god. Laban could not touch Rachel. In the same manner, the power over your family will not touch you when you are in the manner of the cross. Remember God's love is to be appeased with blood. The blood of the lamb which flowed in Jacob, that also flowed through Rachel and made them one flesh, gave her the power and authority to sit on and overcome the household god. *Sit on the god of your household and pour the blood of Jesus on it; that's how you can overcome your household god.*

8. **Laban will never find his household god again.**

   Because she was sitting on it and the way of woman was on her, she became untouchable by the commander or the executor of the household god. Sit on that household god until his presence disappears in your family. Do you know that after this incident, the presence of the household god was never found in her life as well as the life of her children? You may ask, "How do you know that? Potiphar's wife's charge was to destroy Joseph." But because the mother sat on the household god, she repositioned Joseph to a great place in life. I therefore beseech all mothers to spend time to pray for their children and family. When Rachel did it, it had an impact on Joseph, causing him to succeeding. *So, will you?*

I want to move to the next chapter where I am going to discuss the three dimensions of prayer, because to sit on the household god is not child's play. You must sit on it prayerfully, at night, during the day, and let them know that you are now in charge spiritually. Let us go to the next chapter to see what is itching in my spirit. We will then pray there.

Chapter 10
The Three Dimensions of Prayer

Most people just pray, which is great, but there is more to this subject of prayer. I have read a lot about prayer, and what I have concluded is that most people write on prayer activity, but do not really take you through the dimensions. I was privileged to be given this revelation. I am so excited about sharing it with you today.

I was in Toronto, Canada, and was convening a conference for my friend Dr. George, when God began to pour His word into my spirit. So, one morning, during our morning prayer, God just opened my mind to this dimension which I had never seen from His word:

1. **The first dimension is just prayer.**
   All religions pray, everyone prays, and you will find people that will tell you that they have been praying and nothing works. In reality, we live in an era where we have software updates, but people do not update their prayer life. People are still reciting old prayers and expect that they will have answers. Some people are tired of investing energy and passion towards prayer, meanwhile the Bible clearly states that when Jesus prayed in the garden of Gethsemane, He prayed until His sweat became blood (Luke 22:44). If the son of God can pray this way, what makes you believe that you will pray unconcerned and yet expect a great answer? Prayer is the only way that connects human beings to the heavenly decision. Prayer allows you to enter into the corridors of heaven and make your case.
   We live in the age where Muslims pray **five times** a day and where Jews prays **three times** daily, **four times** daily on the

Sabbath and during most Jewish holidays, and **five times** on Yom Kippur. We were on a flight going to Tel Aviv one time for a Holy Land tour; the flight was a 13-hour flight and there were some Jewish rabbis who got up and faced Jerusalem from the sky and prayed every time they needed to pray. I found it very impressive as I observed them. I found it fascinating to see that people are devoted to just the first dimension of prayer, which is simple prayer. Pray without ceasing. You are doing well if you are praying simple prayers, but you can do better than that. This is the first dimension, to just to pray. God can only be connected to us through prayer; Paul told the Philippians not to worry about anything, but to pray in all things, to pray and the peace of God would keep their minds and hearts in Christ Jesus.

> *"⁶Do not be anxious about anything, but in every situation, by prayer and petition, with thanksgiving, present your requests to God. ⁷ And the peace of God, which transcends all understanding, will guard your hearts and your minds in Christ Jesus."* Philippians 4:6-7

The peace of God to keep your heart and mind is in your prayer and your faithfulness to prayer. In other words, you will have the peace of mind that surpasses all understanding in prayer.

Another time, James said to us in James 5:13 that if anyone is afflicted, let him pray. Prayer is the prescription of heaven to anyone afflicted. Affliction is part of life, where we find ourselves afflicted by people, demons, witches and sorcerers, yet the remedy for the affliction is not telling people how bad it is and how angry you are. Instead, it is in your ability to pray and move the heavens by your prayer.

I was invited one day to pray for a family. As we began praying, the power of God came down, things began to happen, and the mother started weeping under the power of the Holy Spirit. As soon as we were done, I immediately left the place because I was feeling dizzy under the power of the Spirit of God. There is power in prayer, yet the enemy has made believers believe that there is no power in prayer.

If anyone among you is afflicted let him pray, it's as simple as that. Pray Until the Burden is Uplifted from your Spirit (PUBUS). You can also use the PUSH strategy as we saw before: PRAY UNTIL SOMETHING HAPPENS.

Your prayer has the resulting effect of your peace of mind, knowing that God is in control. If you want peace of mind, just pray and take your issue into God's hands. Someone asked me why they should pray seeing that God knows everything already. He is the omniscient, all-knowing God. I said to her that yes, He knows everything, even the end from the beginning, but He still wants us to communicate with Him; prayer is communication with your maker. It's not because He doesn't know, but by telling Him you are also building a relationship with Him that is based not on religion, but on personal experience. Remember, our Lord Jesus Christ is the son of God, yet when He came on earth, He never stopped praying to God. He never stopped communicating with God because He had a mission on earth. *So, we need to also practice what Jesus Christ did?* As long as we are alive, we don't have to stop praying, for we are still on our assignment here on earth. Jesus prayed and said on the cross, "It is finished," and after that, he died (John 19:30). We don't have to stop our communication with God, because it builds our relationship with our Father in Heaven. Let the Lord's will be done on earth. And it is His will that we partake of his strength through prayer. He said to: "**ask, and it will be given to you; seek, and you will find; knock, and it will be opened to you** (Luke 11:9)." All of these can be achieved when there is a fervent prayer.

To pray is great and it shows that at least you know there is someone bigger than you are. To pray means you are in the first dimension of prayer. In 2 Corinthians 12:2, Paul talks to us about being taken to the third heaven; to pray is the activity of the first heaven. If you pray it is to acknowledge that there is a higher power than you. All religions pray and that is not beyond anything. People have written prayers, dictated prayers, sung prayers; there are all sorts of prayers out there. However, the best prayer is the one that comes from your heart in all sincerity and honesty. I have learned something: that sincerity is not proof of truth, because you can be sincerely wrong.

David said in Psalms 109:4, **"For my love they are my adversaries: but I give myself unto prayer."** Get to this level if ever you want to stand strong in life against your adversaries. Your prayer works in the first heaven. Give yourself to prayer.

2. The Second Dimension is Warfare

Ephesians 6: 10-20 reads:

¹⁰ Finally, be strong in the Lord and in his mighty power. ¹¹ Put on the full armor of God, so that you can take your stand against the devil's schemes. ¹² For our struggle is not against flesh and blood, but against the rulers, against the authorities, against the powers of this dark world and against the spiritual forces of evil in the heavenly realms. ¹³ Therefore put on the full armor of God, so that when the day of evil comes, you may be able to stand your ground, and after you have done everything, to stand. ¹⁴ Stand firm then, with the belt of truth buckled around your waist, with the breastplate of righteousness in place, ¹⁵ and with your feet fitted with the readiness that comes from the gospel of peace. ¹⁶ In addition to all this, take up the shield of faith, with which you can extinguish all the flaming arrows of the evil one. ¹⁷ Take the helmet of salvation and the sword of the Spirit, which is the word of God.
¹⁸ And pray in the Spirit on all occasions with all kinds of prayers and requests. With this in mind, be alert and always keep on praying for all the Lord's people. ¹⁹ Pray also for me, that whenever I speak, words may be given me so that I will fearlessly make known the mystery of the gospel, ²⁰ for which I am an ambassador in chains. Pray that I may declare it fearlessly, as I should.

I was sleeping on the 31st night of December 2017, and I remembered before sleeping I was just asking God some questions concerning my ministry. I told the Lord I was very tired of just preaching. *Pass me not oh gentle savior, hear my humble heart!* I believe you know the hymn, right? It is just a powerful hymn. I had a dream, and in the dream, I saw myself in a big meeting. It was like a crusade, there were a lot of people, and when I got there I was told to sit at the back of the crowd. I saw my pastor, Dr. Ralph come in and take me from the crowd, and he said, "Khalala, you are going to minister to these people today." So I asked myself, *what am I going to talk about, oh God?* And clearly, I heard the voice of the Master! He said to me, **"Turn your Bible to Ephesians 6; we do not wrestle against flesh and blood."** He said to me, **"Flesh and blood are not your problem."** That is where I want to begin today, *the second dimension of prayer, which is Warfare.*

Paul clearly describes that we do not fight against flesh and blood, which means that what you see is not your problem. There is something behind every flesh and blood. Most of us respond only to the flesh and blood and do not look beyond the flesh and blood, to fight the spirit behind everything.

To warfare, what does it really mean? The role of warfare is to spiritually fight your opponents until they release what belongs to you. This can take some time before the opponents declare themselves out of the fight because you have gained the territory or taken over.

Warfare has to do with the territory lost in the spiritual realm. When you begin to warfare you gain your place and your territory. Warfare is the activity of the second heaven. We fight not with flesh and blood, but against spiritual hosts in heavenly places. Warfare takes place in the second heaven. Check what the Bible says in Revelation 12:7: that there was a war in heaven, not where God is, but the second heaven, and the devil was defeated. You must warfare and stand your ground, because Satan is angry; he wants to remove you and make sure that you are out of your territory. *Be your territorial commander. Never allow the devil to defeat you. Remember, Satan never succeeded after testing our Lord Jesus Christ because Jesus stood His ground!* Can you imagine How Satan could give Jesus Christ, the son of the living God, all the nations, power and glory on earth, forgetting that He created heaven and the earth and all that is in it? The Lord has given *us* the dominion to subdue the earth. Jesus never ever gave Satan his territory, so do not give up your territory to the devil. Remember, Satan came to steal, to kill and to destroy (John 10:10). *Stand your grounds! Pursue, overtake, and overcome him.*

How do you gain control over what you do not see, because they are not flesh and blood?

Look at the list of the fighting match:
1. We fight against principalities
2. We fight against powers
3. We fight against wicked spirits in heavenly places
4. We fight against rulers of darkness of this age
5. We fight against spiritual forces

When you are in a fight, you must engage and take on your opponent. You must let him know that you have decided and are determined to carry the fight until you get your victory – that you are not willing to give up now.

The time my wife and I could not have a child I will never forget. As mentioned, my wife had several failed pregnancies. During the last one, she had to go through surgery to remove the dead infant in her womb. When we got out of there, I was mad in my spirit and I did not say a word to anybody. I waited and believed God for the next pregnancy. The next one came after a year; it took me three months of warfare. In the beginning of the pregnancy I spent three hours each night in my living room fighting with the devil and against witchcraft to leave my child alone. *Hmmm!* There was another thing that made me upset. One day we went to a convention and some people (I will not mention their names) told me that the Lord had told them that my wife had to come with me on the trip so they could find a solution for her. They told me to drink a solution they had mixed up and give it to my spouse. My spirit was not in agreement so I rejected it. Just because something comes from a man of God doesn't not mean you have to take it, especially when your spirit does not agree. I stood in warfare for three hours every night faithfully to break that power over my child and on December 9th, 2013 at 10:20 a.m., my boy was born, 4.10 kilos. Praise God! Again, I named him Win Prince Khalala because I won the battle. Now this boy is called Win; what I did was give a name to my victory. Remember Jacob also renamed his son Benjamin, which meant "laughter."

When you come to this dimension, you are dealing with forces of darkness that nobody sees yet the impact on everyday life is so real.

Every warfare demands three things in order to be effective:

1. **You need to have information about your enemy.**
   You need to know who you are dealing with; in Luke 8:30, Jesus asked the man who was possessed, "What is your name?" The name He asked for was not the man's name, but

the spirit that possessed the man. In other words, you must identify them. You need to know who you are facing so you can know how to deal with them. I saw the movie *American Sniper,* which really blessed my soul. It was when the Americans were fighting the Vietnamese, and the Vietnamese had a sniper that was so skilled that he killed a lot of Americans without them knowing where he was firing his weapon from. So, the army recalled a sniper who was in his retirement to stalk the Vietnamese sniper – a stalker stalking the stalker. This American sniper spent a lot of days just trying to learn the habits of this Vietnamese sniper. In the course of time the Vietnamese sniper would come out from his hiding place to stretch, so the American sniper now knew how to get him. He shot him when he was coming out to stretch and that was the end of most of the confrontation. You must know your enemy. That will require you to study the pattern of things, how and when they happen.

2. **You need to know the strength of your enemy.**
   What is the strength of your enemy? How far can your enemy go? How powerful is your enemy? How long has your enemy been in existence? Similarly, Jesus Christ asked the demon what his name was and he replied, "My name is Legion (Mark 5:9)." The amazing thing that happened was that the demons begged Jesus not to cast them out of the region, but to send them to the swine. The swine then rushed to the sea. Then one day, Jesus was crossing with His disciples to the other side of the water and it happened that Jesus was sleeping and a great storm arose to the point that the boat was being filled with water. Jesus was sleeping so

the disciples woke Him up and said, "Master, Master we are perishing (Luke 8:24)." The Bible continued that Jesus awoke from His sleep and rebuked the wind. He knew that the wind that was in the sea was not a normal wind, that it was sponsored by the demons that He had cast out that went into the sea. Though the devil thought he was arousing the kind of wind to threaten Jesus's destiny and the disciples, it was rebuked. Jesus rebuked the wind. That was the only instance Jesus rebuked the wind, because that wind was not from the weather network, but from the pit of the hell. The devil was up to something, but Jesus rebuked the wind.

3. **You need to know the habits of your enemy.**

   What are the patterns and ways that your enemies operate, ways that they take to do what they have to do? One thing I might mention here is that when Jesus asked the man possessed in Luke chapter 5, "What is your name?" The demon inside the man said, "My name is legion." In other words, can you imagine that people know you are called so and so, yet there is another name that is out there that you are called? The man responded to Jesus' question that his name was legion. Legion was a military term to signify the number of soldiers who were in that group. Usually a legion included 3,000 horsemen and 3,000 footmen, but that is not what I want to get into. What I really want to note is that the legion did not want to go away from that community because they knew how people thought and behaved. You must know the habit of your enemy. Your enemy studies you, takes time to roam like a roaring lion planning to see how to deal with you. Now that you know this, whenever you are engaged in a fight of this kind, you must keep at it until your spirit receives a release that your enemy has backed off. The devil is a master in this area, and the Apostle Paul said not to be ignorant of his devices less he gains advantage over us (2 Corinthians 2:11).

Check this out – Revelation 12:7-11:

> *7 And there was war in heaven: Michael and his angels fought against the dragon; and the dragon fought and his angels,*
>
> *8 And prevailed not; neither was their place found any more in heaven.*
>
> *9 And the great dragon was cast out, that old serpent, called the Devil, and Satan, which deceived the whole world: he was cast out into the earth, and his angels were cast out with him.*
>
> *10 And I heard a loud voice saying in heaven, now is come salvation, and strength, and the kingdom of our God, and the power of His Christ: for the accuser of our brethren is cast down, which accused them before our God day and night.*
>
> *11 And they overcame him by the blood of the Lamb, and by the word of their testimony; and they loved not their lives unto the death.*

When you are engaged in warfare, you climb to the second heaven and gain what the Lord has for you. So many of us pass on the fight because it takes time. I will develop this in an upcoming chapter; I'm excited!

Again, Peter the Apostle said: "…your adversary the devil walks about like a roaring lion, seeking whom he may devour. Resist him (1 Peter 5:8-9)."

My beloved, you must make up your mind to warfare, and gain your place. You have been switched and moved without knowing that someone orchestrated your move. You think all is well, but bit by bit you are being moved over from the place of your calling. Warfare in the night, warfare in the day, and let the enemy know that you mean business.

Let me go to the last dimension of prayer. I feel like a pregnant woman who is ready to deliver; I mean, I have a lot to say!

3. **The third dimension is wresting.**
   To wrestle is to maintain your opponents at a position where you gain control, whereby they no longer control you, but you begin to control them. To wrestle is the activity of the third heaven; wrestling is the way you get the will of God get done on earth.

   Luke 22:42 reads, "Father, if you are willing, take this cup from me; yet not my will, but yours be done." Not my will but your will be done; if this is true for Jesus then it is also true for you. If you do not pay attention you could depend on your own will or the will of the enemy without even knowing it.

   He wrestled until the sweat became drops of blood. Wow, what an investment! *You mean he sweated in prayer?* In this dimension, everything you've got is to be incorporated in your wrestling – your energy, your passion, your hands, your seed, your voice and your entire body movement.

At this stage you want to put the opponent under your control. You must arise with force and passion to get this job done. You see, I can pray for you, but I can never wrestle and warfare for you, because it is a principle that no one will fight in any other dimension for you. Remember Jacob wrestled with the man; that's God. Jacob did it for himself and after, his name was changed to Israel. The key thing is to wrestle to get your possessions.

Check this one out. In the story of Hannah in the book of 1 Samuel, after all these times going to Shiloh, she had to go into a wrestling match for herself for things to begin to change. The role wrestling plays is that it places your opponents in the position where you have control over them until they declare that they can no longer continue to fight you. This can take some time before the opponent declares him or herself out of the fight because you have taken control.

There are things you will solve by prayer and there are other things that your prayer is not enough for.

In Matthew chapter 7, Jesus took James, John and Peter on a high mountain. Jesus was transfigured there and two people showed up with Him. They were Moses and Elijah, the prayer warriors of their time. In Exodus 34, Moses wrestled with God for the glory until his face was shining in the glory of God and even his own people could not look at his face. As for Elijah, the

Bible describes him as a man with passion, and in 1 Kings 17, he prayed that there would be no rain for three years and a half. On that day of transfiguration on the mountain, not only did prayerful warriors appear, but there was another thing that happened. Do you remember in Deuteronomy 32:52, when the Lord told Moses that he would see the land, but not enter it? I believe that's why the devil was contending with the angel for the body of Moses (Jude 9:22-24). When you wrestle, even after you die you will see where God is taking you; you will be there. Moses' feet were in the Promised Land. Who told you that it cannot be done? *It can!*

Wrestling requires three things for you to be effective in your wrestling, unless you want to waste your time and energy.

1. **In order to wrestle effectively you need energy.**
   This may sound very simple, but how many people pray while tired? Again, the Bible says that when Jesus was praying in the garden of Gethsemane, His sweat became like drops of blood. You do not sweat unless you exert force which requires energy.
   You can't wrestle with an opponent when you are tired. Invest energy; you must be in your best mental and physical form. We invest our energy in matters that really don't push our life to the dimension that we want. God cannot use a tired body. My Pastor, Dr. Ralph Dartey always told us as young ministers, "You must get in your best shape and form. Invest your energy in prayer, wrestling prayer, to activate the deeper dimension of your life."

2. **In order to wrestle effectively you need skills**

   A wrestler who has skills will have advantage over his enemy. You will not need physical skills, but spiritual skills to know how your enemy moves. Wrestling is a sport of moves: dangling from left to right, knowing how to hold your enemy, having a grip on him, and other technical strategies. You need to know how to get a grip on your opponent when he moves from one way to another. If you watch a wrestling match you will see that what the two fighters do best is move from one place to another. You must know how to corner your enemy and get a grip on them. It takes skills to juggle with your opponents. Remember that the enemy was once an angel of light, and then became the serpent of old, the devil, the wicked one, the angel of darkness. All of this is to show you how skillful your enemy is, and he never wants you to have a grip on him, because once you have a grip on your opponent it becomes easy to bring him down. Remember in 1 Samuel chapter 17, David had wrestling skills and he was able to kill and defeat Goliath with a stone!

   Let me give you an example here. When you begin to have a great prayer life, for a while the enemy will send you programs and things to disturb your rhythm in wrestling. The devil will bring you a lucrative job as a distraction to disrupt your rhythm in the wrestling match.

3. **In order to be effective in wrestling you need light.**

   You need light; what I mean is that you need revelation. You need something that your opponent has no idea of, but that you knew all along. Paul in the book of Ephesians 1:18, when praying for them, said: "I pray that the eyes of your heart may be enlightened in order that you may know the hope to which he has called you, the riches of his glorious inheritance in his holy people." You must wrestle with opened eyes so that you see your enemy the same way he sees you. Remember, the Bible tells us time and again to watch and pray. To watch will help God reveal things to you, whether physical or spiritual things. Again, we do not wrestle against flesh and blood; you must be able to go beyond flesh and blood in order to pin point your opponent and get your victory.

I have a word from the Lord for you: wrestle until you put the enemy under your control and you are in charge. Hannah wrestled until no one could hear her voice clearly, she sounded like someone who took something, as if she was drunk. Eli asked whether she was drunk and she replied "No, my lord, I am a woman of sorrowful spirit. I have drunk neither wine nor intoxicating drink, but have poured out my soul before the Lord (1 Samuel 1:15)."

Wrestling takes you straight to the third heaven, where you wrestle for His will to be done in your life. Whose will are you living with right now? Is it the will of God, the will of people, your own will, the will of your enemy, or the will of wickedness?

You must take control of your destiny; things are happening without your knowledge. It looks like you are a stranger in your life. You are discovering things just like everyone. Let that be no more. Wrestle for the will of the Father to be done in your life. When I left the organization I used to work with, one pastor stood on the pulpit of the church I had planted and said to the congregation that, since I had left, they were giving me three months and that I would shut down the ministry I had just started. With those three months they gave me, what they did was build a three-month cycle around me so that every three months, I had to feel like I'm starting the ministry over. Until one day, in a dream, I was coming from a trip and saw a man coming from our church building. There was light inside the building, but he had the keys of the church. I saw him lock the church and run away with the keys. Meanwhile there was so much light in the building, nobody from the street could miss the light in the building. I confronted the man in the dream and he started running away. So, I had to pursue him. Now let me tell you the meaning of that dream. When people came to our church, they loved it. The presence of God was present, but people never stayed. It was not about the program organized in the church, but there was a force in the community that stood to close the doors of the church in the spirit realm. I remember one day we were praying and we were only three people. From midnight to 2 a.m. there was the presence of witchcraft inside the church, and the witch stood by the door and watched us. When she discovered that I saw her, she ran away, and from that day people began to come inside the church and stayed. It was in that moment that God inspired me to do a program called Revival in my City. Last year was the first edition. The man of God who came took us to higher dimensions of prayer, warfare and wrestling. I do not want you to confuse these three things; prayer, warfare and wrestling are all not the same. There is a big difference in their terminologies.

Dear beloved, wrestle until what heaven has promised you becomes a reality. Jacob, who carried so many prophecies, got to the point that he wrestled against the angel of the Lord for a blessing. I said it the previous chapter that he was willing to fight in order to be blessed.

Chapter 11
The Money is Not in the Bank,
But is Stuck in Someone's Mouth

Matthew 17:24-27:

24 After Jesus and his disciples arrived in Capernaum, the collectors of the two-drachma temple tax came to Peter and asked, "Doesn't your teacher pay the temple tax?"
25 "Yes, he does," he replied.
When Peter came into the house, Jesus was the first to speak. "What do you think, Simon?" he asked. "From whom do the kings of the earth collect duty and taxes—from their own children or from others?"
26 "From others," Peter answered.
"Then the children are exempt," Jesus said to him. 27 "But so that we may not cause offense, go to the lake and throw out your line. Take the first fish you catch; open its mouth and you will find a four-drachma coin. Take it and give it to them for my tax and yours."

I was almost finished writing this book; I was on the last chapter when the Holy Spirit prompted me to add this chapter. God indeed enlightens us with His word of knowledge and he never leaves us until we finish the assignment He has given us. Now, let's proceed.

The story goes like this. The temple tax collectors asked the disciples if their Master did not believe in paying taxes. Today most people will fail on tax issues. We get the money and hide it from everyone else. We put it in a bank that does not check the source of the funds and when we die, banks lock the funds for no one to use it. That is wrong, not good at all. Learn to give your contribution as much as you can. I will leave it at that.

Jesus told Peter in Matthew chapter 17, when asked about taxes, that he did pay taxes and wanted Peter to know that he would not cheat the system.

I want us to look at couple of things in the light of this scripture.

1. These people had the audacity to come and ask the Word made flesh tax money.

They thought that Jesus did not pay the temple tax; He said destroy this temple and I will rebuild it in three days. What audacity they had, thinking that Jesus would fall for their little scheme. You know, most people will try things to make sure you get stuck by the question they ask you. The question was not about money, but to trick him. Beware brethren.

2. The money is not in the bank.

The more I read Matthew 17, the more I come to appreciate what Jesus is trying to show us here when asked about the tax money. He told Peter to go to the river. "What are you trying to tell me here, Lord?" – Peter should have asked. Go to the sea? You do not get money in the sea, money is at the bank. Jesus did not send Peter to the bank, but to the sea. If you read the gospel you will come to realize that Jesus had people with substance who supported Him.

The gospel of Luke actually writes about and even gives the names of these women who supported Jesus with their substance. Yet, Jesus did not ask Peter to go to any of His partners, but to the sea; why?

I strongly believe that there is a revelation here that will lift up our life. This fish that Jesus is telling Peter about had the audacity and courage to swallow Jesus' tax money. If the fish was not afraid to swallow Jesus' tax money, then what about you?

3. Why is it that this fish had money in his mouth?

How come the fish never choked or died from having things in its mouth in the water?

"... go to the lake and throw out your line. Take the first fish you catch; open its mouth and you will find a four-drachma coin. Take it and give it to them for my tax and yours."

Here, I strongly believe that, just like Daniel when he began to pray, his answer was sent, but there was a demonic interruption over that city because of him (Daniel 10:13). This is what heaven has sent to you that has to pass through people and things. Jesus's tax money had to pass through the fish, but the fish swallowed it and would not give it up. The Bible says in the book of Jonas that God sent a big fish and he swallowed the prophet Jonas. If fish can swallow money from prophets and Jesus, your family may have been swallowed by the witchcraft of your village and country. *Arise in prayer, somebody.*

4. How come this fish was not afraid to swallow Jesus' tax money?

The fact that you are a child of God does not mean that the devil will be afraid to touch what belongs to you. The fish was audacious to keep Jesus' money, and to live in the lake until Peter used his skills to get it out of the lake to take the money back. You would think that money would be in the bank. You keep submitting applications to be approved by the bank, yet you must deal with the spirit that swallows things in your family.

Do you have any idea how much of your stuff has been under the water? Jesus' tax money was under the water; while walking, Peter had no idea that his tax money was also under the water.

The solution is not always in going to borrow more to cover whatever need you have. You need to roll up your sleeves and deal with the spirit that swallows your success, your promotion, your money, etc. Here you are in debt; meanwhile, there is a demon playing with your money under the water.

He was walking on dry land, but his tax money was under the waters. It took a revelation from Jesus to bring it out. Jesus had the anointing to know about and locate the funds under the waters, specifically in the mouth of the fish. But Peter's fishing skills materialized the anointing that Jesus had about the tax money.

One time, Peter went fishing and all that night he caught nothing. Jesus told him to cast his net for a catch, and Peter answered that they had toiled all night and caught nothing (Luke 5:5). Jesus was telling Peter that last night was the season for nothing; today begins a day where your net will have more than you ever thought of in life. Whoever is hiding your money in some place, I command your skills to arise and get it out for you in the name of Jesus. Can you imagine how this little fish took in its mouth what belonged to Jesus, the son of the living God? Have you ever tried to get something from a living fish? It will definitely be a fight because they do not want you to touch them or to open their mouth. But listen to what Jesus said to Peter: "open its mouth." *Open its mouth, take it, and do not be afraid or feel sorry for the fish and the things in its mouth.* This is where your tax money to settle the debt was freed. You see, if I can talk about Peter, assuming that Peter lived in this modern society, Peter would have gone to the bank and submitted an application for another loan. When it comes to finances, the devil does not joke with that. He can try all the possible means to prevent believers from having their financial breakthrough, because he thinks that they will do greater and mightier things on earth, relating this to the scripture written in Genesis that we should be fruitful and multiply, dominate and subdue the earth. Fight that fish, open its mouth and take your money to pay your debt, to build your business or project. The money to buy your home is not in the bank. Take a deep time of prayer to command the fish – that has been there to swallow your life – to release it.

Think with me for a moment, why did Jesus see that there was something in the mouth of a fish somewhere in the sea? Why only in the sea? And why not buried, why not kept somewhere inside someone's house?

5. Open its mouth and take it.

We do not know the size of this fish; however, we know Peter's determination. He was not willing to go back without getting the tax money.

Think about the laboring process he used to get the money from the fish – going to the river, throwing his net, finding the first fish and not the second one – and the first opening its mouth, ready to give out the four pieces of money! He took it and payed the tax for himself *and* Jesus.

Among Jesus' disciples was a tax collector; how come he never advised the Lord about it? If you think people will give you what you need in life then you are kidding yourself. You must take it from its mouth.

The devil has swallowed stuff that you have no idea of. As long as there was no demand, nobody knew that something had taken the money that belonged to them.

Can you imagine that the money to pay the tax was not in the bank, but in the mouth of some fish? Who has taken what is yours in this life? Nobody by natural eyes or natural means could see that the tax money was under the river in some fish's mouth. This tells me that there are forces that have swallowed people's promotion, wealth, marriage, success, progress, happiness, jobs, children, etc. It seems as if there is no money yet Heaven has already sent you the provision. It could be that the marine spirit of the place you live in has taken it and hidden it. That's why the Bible says in Isaiah chapter 45 that God will give unto us the riches in the secret places and the treasures of darkness.

If Jesus had not been there during that period of tax collection, Peter would have gone to get a second job in order to cover the cost of the taxes that were required of him. You have a choice to believe it, or just think that life will be good someday.

I am tired of the gospel of babysitting me; give me the real meat, and let me fight after those forces that are resisting me and standing in my way in this life.

In Daniel chapter 10, Daniel was living in Persia, and when he began praying, heaven sent the answer to his prayers, but there was a spirit that stood in the heavenly places controlling the activities of the believers. When that spirit saw that God had given the answer to Daniel's prayer, he decided to stop and fight the angel that carried Daniel's answers until the 21st day! *Hmmm...* what does you mean, Pastor?

In the spirit realm 21 days of prayer breaks resistance that your prayers have encountered. Allow me to repeat the statement from a man of God that blessed me tremendously: "Persistent breaks Resistance."

So long as the word of God says knock and it shall be opened unto you, then you must knock until the door is opened unto to you. When this is done, no demon can keep messing with your life, children and family. How come things happen the way they happen? Is it coincidence? I do not think so! Something bizarre has been happening yet we let it go and say, "Well, things will get better." Who told you? You must engage in spiritual battle and confront the forces of retardation, resistance and forces that have been in the family to close up all the doors and leave you stranded. *Only warfare prayer will help you to win.*

Some time ago, I heard a story that left me asking questions. It was about a man who went to steal someone's computer and sound system. The owner of the stolen items did not say a word, but instead did something, by spiritually commanding bees. Yes, bees! That's right, you heard me well! He sent the bees to arrest the thief and bring him to where he committed his crime. If a mere man could command that spiritually and it came to pass, then how much more a child of God? I therefore decree and declare that all forces of darkness that have taken any treasure of yours – be it money, career, finances, marriage, children, etc. – and have hidden them under the waters, be released unto you in the name of Jesus Christ of Nazareth. Shout a good *Amen!*

Peter would have worked hard to get the tax money to pay off, yet Jesus said to him, and I'm paraphrasing, "Peter, just go to the river, catch a fish and open its mouth." You know what, for you to open the mouth of a living fish is a battle, yet you must fight to open its mouth and take the money. It was right there as soon as he was able to open its mouth. Beloved, you must fight to get that which is yours. The last time I checked I read the word of God saying to Joshua to be strong and courageous! You also need to be strong, bold, and fight to get the treasures out of its mouth. They have taken what is yours, do not just stay there and watch by using the common words, "God knows." No! You need to fight in prayer to get what is stuck in someone's mouth, pocket or office. There are people who are supposed to give you your tax money yet they are busy spending it. *Command it to be released.* When you pray fervently, remember the Bible in Joel 2:25-26 mentions that whatever the locust has eaten will be vomited out!

Prayer is answered in three realms:

1. Physical Realm

When you pray, God touches someone to give you what you have prayed for. One day, I was praying to God to give me some money which I needed to get something done quickly, and when I came back, I found a check in the mail that someone had sent me. The amount sent was exactly what I needed to cover my need. I strongly believe that one day when you pray, God will touch your heart to bless someone. One day as I began to pray, God touched my heart to encourage someone with a text message. As soon as the person received my text message, she said, "How did you know that I was going through this at this particular moment?"

Your prayer has been heard from heaven, but the evil person on earth has refused to release the heavenly package that belongs to you. The human will is so strong that it could obstruct the will of God. I command everyone who is supposed to release what God has ordained for you to do so in Jesus' Name. Around 2005, I did not have the indenture for the land, so one day God told me to do something: to call my friend who had the same problem I was dealing with. My friend then sent me what his lawyer had worked on so that I could follow the same procedure that his lawyer did. I called my friend and did exactly as it was commanded to me by heavenly vision. However, in the office where my stuff was being processed, there was a gentleman who took my file and wouldn't do anything until I gave him an unreasonable request. I took it to prayer and wrestled against that human will that stood in my way. And blessed be the name of the Lord who gave me victory! There are blessings that God has released due to your prayer, but there is human will, not to mention witches, who will stand in your way. Nevertheless, the good news is that you can rise up and move them out of your way.

2. Angelic Realm

As mentioned, in the book of Daniel, the angel of God came to Daniel and said to him that from the first day he decided to pray, he – the angel of God – was sent to him; however, he encountered the prince of Persia that withstood him for 21 days. Looking at this story, I strongly believe that there are spirits that control the sky above us. Daniel thought that the king that was ruling was responsible for the kingdom. *No way*; it was the prince of Persia that controlled the traffic of all individuals in that country. There are witches and sorcerers that have a mandate to control the movement from your life to heaven. They do not want you to receive anything from heaven. Their job is to keep you in your current status until you get frustrated and quit praying. Take charge over every demonic activity that has been placed above you to control what you must receive and what you must get to move on in life.

3. The Will Realm

1 Samuel 1:12-18:

> *12 As she kept on praying to the LORD, Eli observed her mouth.*
> *13 Hannah was praying in her heart, and her lips were moving but her voice was not heard. Eli thought she was drunk 14 and said to*

her, "How long are you going to stay drunk? Put away your wine."

15 "Not so, my lord," Hannah replied, "I am a woman who is deeply troubled. I have not been drinking wine or beer; I was pouring out my soul to the LORD. 16 Do not take your servant for a wicked woman; I have been praying here out of my great anguish and grief."

17 Eli answered, "Go in peace, and may the God of Israel grant you what you have asked of Him."

18 She said, "May your servant find favor in your eyes." Then she went her way and ate something, and her face was no longer downcast.

This realm is for those who bring the will of God to pass regardless of the odds. The Bible told us about it when Jesus was teaching His disciples on how to pray in Matthew 6:9- 13:

Our Father in heaven,
Hallowed be Your name.
Your kingdom come.
Your will be done
On earth as it is in heaven.
Give us this day our daily bread.
And forgive us our debts,
As we forgive our debtors.
And do not lead us into temptation,
But deliver us from the evil one.
For Yours is the kingdom and the power and the glory forever. Amen.

I would like to illustrate this part here: *Your kingdom come and Your will be done on earth as it is in heaven.* Seriously, this verse shows me that in heaven you might be different than what you are on earth.

There are forces that systematically stand in your way to make sure that you never become what heaven has intended for you to be. Being in this realm during prayer could even cause you to not understand the language or the meanings in your prayer. Hannah in 1 Samuel 1:5, as I quoted previously, began to pray to move the will of God because, as the Bible says:

> But to Hannah he gave a double portion because he loved her, and the LORD had closed her womb. Because the LORD had closed Hannah's womb, her rival kept provoking her in order to irritate her.

She prayed to the point that her prayer surpassed human understanding, human comprehension, human psychosis, human psychology and human intellect. The priest, with in his human comprehension, could not understand the degree of Hannah's depth in prayer. So, he then said to Hannah, and I paraphrase, "Woman quit your wine," and she replied, "I have not given myself to wine; I was pouring out my soul to the Lord (1 Samuel 1:14-15)."

PRAYER TIME

<u>Prayer 1</u>

Can you put the book down for a moment and pour your heart out to the Lord?

What is the depth of the burden that you carry?
Father, I bless you for blessing my life with your word today. I thank you for you are the author and finisher of my faith.

Father, your word is active in my life; therefore, I come to your throne room of grace, mercy and favor.

Father I refuse to be stuck at where I am in life today,
Father please let your kingdom come and your will be done in my life as it is in heaven. (I do not want to be in heaven shining and on earth covered by mud.)

Lord Jesus, I know with you every impossibility in my life will become possible. I trust in you, oh Lord, and I acknowledge that whatever is possible in the spiritual realm is also possible in the physical realm.

Please Lord, change my story and give me a new song! AMEN!
(You can sing this hymn: Blessed Assurance by Fanny Crosby.)

Going back to the fish that Jesus told Peter to go and catch then open its mouth to take the 2 pieces of money that would pay the tax for himself and Peter.

Prayer 2

Every fish sent from the demonic world to swallow my breakthrough; I command you to release it in the name of Jesus.

There are fish that are demonic; they will not go eat what every other fish is eating, but they will try to take what is not theirs.

I decree and declare today, may they vomit it out:

They must give up my finances
They must vomit out my promotion
They must release my children and my glory.

These demonic forces swallowed your life so that you never come out, but God has spoken for you and His words are final!

So far as, this fish was able to keep that money; it shows that there are also humans that are manipulated by demonic powers who are sent to swallow and keep that which God has placed for you to pay your taxes. There are people who sit on what belongs to you, because they have power and are in a position of authority to destroy you. They think they can manipulate your destiny. But wait a minute, who do they think they are? What can they do against your life? Remember, God says He will restore unto us what the locust has eaten. So may your soul find a resting place in the Lord. Though the whale swallowed Jonah, what happened when he was in its belly is that he fasted and prayed and found a resting place there. God is with you. Push the devil out of your way. You are blessed.

CHAPTER 12
War Broke Out – You Are at War

Revelation 12:7-9 NKJV:

> *[7] Then war broke out in heaven. Michael and his angels fought against the dragon, and the dragon and his angels fought back. [8] But he was not strong enough, and they lost their place in heaven. [9] The great dragon was hurled down—that ancient serpent called the devil, or Satan, who leads the whole world astray. He was hurled to the earth, and his angels with him.*

I was in Calgary, Alberta, Canada, when the revelation of this verse hit my spirit. We were going for a pastors' development week with our organization, Transforming Life Centre International. My spirit was impregnated with the revelation of the word of God. I started writing, but my mind was moving faster than my hands. I could not keep up with the pace of my spirit. How many of you know what I am talking about?

Before I go on, I would like to ask a few questions:

1. Why is it that out of all the places in this life the devil decided to start a war in heaven?

If you want to start a war, please start it in the place that you can have an advantage to win, not a place that you know will be very difficult or impossible for you to win in. If warfare could break out in heaven, then how much more where you and I live? We were bought with the price and that's the blood of Jesus! Remember the bible says we are also a chosen generation, a royal priesthood and holy nation (1 Peter 2:9). This only makes the devil envious about you and me, and therefore, he wants to fight us. You are at war, beloved, and your attitude must change. You can no longer afford to have a disengaged attitude towards prayer or look disengaged and uncommitted in life. **YOU ARE AT WAR!** Be ready to fight whenever there is a fight that comes your way. The Bible says in Ephesians 6 that we should put on the full amour of Christ.

2. Why start a war that you have no chance of winning?

This is amazing! The enemy started a war when he had no chance of winning the battle. When we were younger, we learned to pick our battles; if by any chance they brought someone that was bigger and stronger than we were, we just did not fight. Most people used to play with us when we were younger. They would start to trouble you and their big brothers would be hiding behind. If you reacted towards them, their big brothers would come out to face you.

3. Why would you cause a war to break out when you know you will not be able to win it?

Most of us underestimate the dark world. The devil is patient in his schemes in order to get you. He exerts a lot of patience, more than most believers do; he will wait until he has an opportunity to knock you down.

We are going to look at this in-depth so that we can grasp the full revelation of the word of God. Life moves by revelation. It is the revelation of the word of God that brings us into the victory we are looking for. Having received Jesus is just the beginning of the process; you must now allow God to open your eyes in order to see into the spiritual realm, break forth and be effective in a war of your life.

The enemy tempts us each and every day; however, if we don't respond in prayer, he will take over and subdue us. The scripture admonishes us to pray that we may not enter into temptation. He started war in heaven and thank God Archangel Michael responded to his aggression.

Let us take few minutes to pray and war against the enemy

- Fight for your life and refuse to be subdued, buried, and overtaken by the enemy.
- Refuse to be bounded by the enemy.

Let us get back on our journey!

The majority of people have no idea of what their enemy is capable of doing. The people that want you dead and want you to fail are willing to do things that you have no idea of; some are ready to go perform all kinds of rituals at the cemetery just to get you destroyed. People who are jealous of you are willing to sacrifice whatever it will cost them in order to bring you down or to eliminate you. Sometimes I laugh when I see many believers who do not take their prayer life seriously and declare that the devil cannot overcome them. On what grounds does your declaration stand? Our enemy is willing to go to every length to overcome you and your children. You know something? Some believers complain *a lot* – enough with the complaints and criticism. When your pastor is giving you instructions sometimes what you do is complain and murmur about the instruction given. This is a wrong attitude to have. It is time for you to you listen, arise, and fight the battle before you.

Are you willing to do anything to overtake the war in your family and in your own life?

As we saw previously, Rachel was willing to go the extra mile to the point that she stole the god of her father and sat on it, risking being cursed and dishonored. Yet, she did it in order to be able to see victory in her children. If Rachel had never sat on the god of her family, I strongly believe that the schemes of Joseph's brothers and the wickedness of Potiphar's wife would have killed her son Joseph.

Some people think that the devil is in a war to make friends; if you don't watch out, he will finish you and your family. If you don't take prayer seriously, the devices of the enemy can frame a nice story for your family like, *oh, he could have been a great man, but something happened to him and he died.* That's what the enemy wishes for us, but blessed be the name of the Lord who is our hope, life and everything, the one who has promised us that, we call Him, He will answer! Thanks be to God.

The purpose of war is to subdue and overtake those that you are at war with.

The devil is not trying to possess your body, but to overtake you and overpower you until you give up and let him have his way. We are not at war to make friends, but to take over aggressively. Most people when war breaks out, they do not respond; they sit as spectators and watch; they have a religious way that makes them feel better, but no impact at all. They remain unconcerned and unresponsive to the aggression of the enemy. You must respond to the aggression.

I want to say this, my dear beloved: the enemy always tries to see your response. I don't know if you know how rats operate. They bite you while blowing air on you to sustain the pain, and at the same time, because they do not want you to realize what is going on. That is exactly what the devil does.

Let us look at the 10 facts about war.
Before I proceed to the ten facts about war, I would like you to pay attention to a story that really blessed my life. I have a friend in the army, and one day we were talking about life issues and politics, and he said something that I never thought of and never forgot in my entire life. The statement he made changed the way I see life and things that happen around me. He said, "***War drives the economy.***" Let me just leave it right there.

10 Facts About War:

1. *War is always in direct proportion to what you possess.*

2. *The reason why there is war in your life is because you carry something that someone is coveting.*
3. *There is no mercy in war; if you mess around you get shot.*

4. *You must aggressively fight to win, not just maintain.*

5. *War is an indication that there are precious things there.*

6. *Nobody reveals his plans at war.*

7. *Secrecy and strategy are the two ingredients to bring victory in a war.*
   o The enemy never reveals his plans on how to attack and destroy you, yet believers sometimes reveal theirs by talking too much and opening up their lives like a book. So, the enemy gets the chance to read and know when and how they are going to get you and destroy you. Remember, the devil came to steal, to kill and to destroy. When Satan comes, he comes with strategies that can lure you. So, let us be as wise as the serpent. War is a strategy; keep your strategy! Remember that our Lord Jesus Christ and David used their anointed strategies in their wars and won!

8. *War is fought for victory, not for fun.*
   o Nobody goes to war for fun or just to see what they can do. The purpose is to subdue your enemies.

9. *War demands a great sacrifice*
   o There was a war movie I watched some time ago. What I realized in the movie was that sometimes, the enemy has to walk and crawl simply just to get you. I strongly believe that at times your enemy goes beyond all means just to get what they want from you. I know this is funny, but let me mention it: Jesus said, be watchful of false

prophets because they are wolves dressed in the sheep skin (Matthew 7:15). You mean to tell me that this wolf is so smart that he ate the flesh yet saved the skin to use it to get the sheep? I found that very interesting.

10. *The reason there is war is because there is an enemy that is aiming at you to bring you down at all costs.*

o You must respond to war that breaks out against you in all facets of your life. You cannot afford to keep looking at things with a casual mindset. Remember, the Bible says in 1 Peter 5:8-9, "Be sober, be vigilant; because your adversary the devil walks about like a roaring lion, seeking whom he may devour. Resist him…" *Resist him!* In fact, I love that the only way to break the roaring lion is to resist him, for when you do, he shall flee from you (James 4:7).

The words used here are "resist him." This word comes from the word "resistance," an electric element and a property that tells you how well a circuit prevents electrons from flowing through the material when a voltage is applied. The resistance in a particular circuit depends on the components/materials and how they are interconnected.

The basic rules of how you calculate the total resistance in a circuit are as follows[4]:

---

[4] George John Stringer. *Elements of Electricity and Electro-Chemistry.* Cambridge, UK. Cambridge University Press, 2015.

$$R_{TOTAL} = R_1 + R_2 \cdots R_n$$

$$\frac{1}{R_{TOTAL}} = \frac{1}{R_1} + \frac{1}{R_2} \cdots \frac{1}{R_n}$$

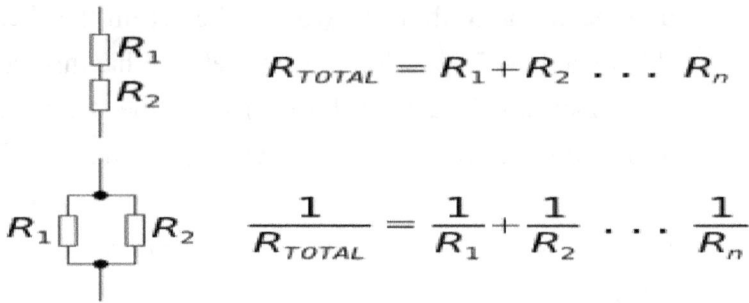

To resist here is to apply necessary force to stand against what the enemy is bringing your way. I like what one gentleman said, that a resistance is just like gravity; without it you will fall out. Similarly, resistance helps you not to blow up when high pressure is applied. Resist him – apply enough force to his pressure so that you do not break. Most people do not match up their prayers to the pressure the devil applies to their lives. Sooner or later they break down and give up.

You must respond to the aggression of witchcraft, enchantment, and wickedness; if you do not respond they will rest over you and rule you.

Be the circuit (believer) that could prevent electrons (Satan) from flowing through the material when a voltage (power & blessings of God) is applied in your life.

One day, a lady dreamed that a huge and fat dark woman was sitting on her in the night. I told her to engage in warfare every night for 30 days to command that witchcraft power to leave her alone. She said to me that whenever the woman came to sit on her in the dream, she would not be able to breathe. Apparently, when she would wake up, she would be short of breath. Sometimes she had panic attacks; her heart would beat very fast, almost like she was about to die.

You *must* respond to the aggression. I do not know how many times I must emphasize it. In the book of Revelation chapter 12, Archangel Michael responded directly to the war that Satan and his cohort brought. Archangel Michael fought to the point that the enemy had no place in heaven anymore. God did not kick him out, but Archangel Michael stood up against him and made sure that he got kicked out.

If you ask many people the type of dreams that they have, it would blow your mind. Yet, they just do nothing and hope things will be better someday. Well, I can tell that things will not change until you rise up in prayer.

Your enemy is willing to do you harm if you do not rise. In response to the lady's dream, I told her to engage in prayer, that if she did not, the enemy would continue to sit on her. The enemy loves to subdue people's families, nations, even churches and communities. *That is why most churches have been closing down; they have the message, but they lack the prayer to drive the message.*

I have one question to ask you, please. When the devil started the war in heaven, where was God? Why didn't He respond? Well, Archangel Michael responded, because it's your responsibility to respond to the attack and the aggression of the enemy.

Respond in fasting, in sowing a seed, in engaging in long warfare prayer. I want to tell you that the enemy is real and we have to engage him. The reason God never responded is because that is the responsibility of the one with whom the devil started the war.

Michael probably said, "No way, I do not want the devil to rule over me. I will defend myself and the kingdom."

Prayer points
1. Fight for your life, and refuse to be subdued, buried or overtaken by the enemy.
2. Do not just watch the enemy bring affliction to your life, family, business and future; respond and declare a warfare night where you will respond to the aggression.
3. What is the demon that your family is fighting? Just to let you know, every family has a demon that pursues them through life.
4. You must resist to the pressure applied on you and your life.
5. Whatever is being prepared in the laboratory of the enemy concerning you, your kids, your ministry and your family must break in Jesus name.

CONCLUSION

In the book of James 5:13, it says: *"Is anyone among you in trouble? Let them pray. Is anyone happy? Let them sing songs of praise."*

I have come to the conclusion of this book, but before I finish, I just want to let you know about one thing. As cited above, James has great advice for us believers. *Is there anyone among you troubled? Let him pray.* Prayer is the only way to get out of the trouble or affliction you are in now. We might try everything in life to ease up our pain, yet prayer is the only solution to human trouble.

There are many things that happen in this life that we can never comprehend, yet they are real and affecting our lives one way or another. I strongly believe that most of the things that affect most people are the things that we never see with our physical eyes, yet they are so powerful. Those things are the cause of people committing suicide, people giving up in life, people living a frustrated life. I am here to tell you that you have to rise up and wrestle not the flesh or blood, but against principalities, rulers of darkness, witchcraft, etc.

Most of us have realize that, there are strange things that happen in our families, yet we have not laid the axe to the root to command that cycle to be broken. Let us have strength in our prayer in order to lift up the people in our families as well as our own lives. We live in an instant generation, where things have become instant in all we do. Previously if you had to send a message to someone, you would have taken a pen and a paper to write a letter and post it. After posting it, the person you sent the letter to would have to wait until the letter is delivered to them. Now it's no longer the same. You can take a picture of the letter and sent it by WhatsApp and instantly they will get it. One more thing or feature is, once they open the message you get to know that they've read the message. This culture has somewhat affected the way Christians relate to God, and how they personally want their prayers be answered by the all-knowing God. Most would want God to respond to their prayers instantly.

Dear beloved, I mention these things to help you be aware of how the devil's schemes are. He's been monitoring our behavior and spreading frustration, depression and oppression so that you will not be able to stand your ground and pray effectively. Again, the Bible says to those who are afflicted or in trouble to pray. Pray until that power is broken. Laban never told Jacob what was going on in his family, about their traditions such as the all-female firstborns having to be married before the younger ones do. He could have asked Jacob whether he would be willing to take both of his daughters before the marriage ceremony. Instead, he allowed him to go through the family cycle so that he could use him as how he wanted to. Be strong and courageous! Be encouraged to stand and fight with your prayers for what is yours. Victory is never given to those who sit and wait, but to those who rise and fight in battle, and wait on God for the victory.

Please say this after me: *it will be done so in my life, I will break free, and I will live a better life. God will cause my enemies to stumble and fall in the name of Jesus. I will succeed and not fall because in Christ I live, move, and have my being, in Jesus' name. Amen.*

Biography of the Writer

Pitchou Khalala was born again in 1992, in Kinshasa, Democratic Republic of Congo. He gave his life to Christ on the very day he heard the audible voice of the Lord calling him to Himself. He heard angelic voices singing in the Heavenly language. His ministry started from the streets of Kinshasa, preaching in open markets early in the morning and in buses. He moved to South Africa to study, where he pursued a college degree in Mechanical Engineering from the Technical College Doorfontein, South Africa, and another college degree from His People Bible College affiliated with the University of Johannesburg, South Africa.

Khalala is a recording artist, songwriter, musician and worship leader, with five albums under his belt. He is married to Nadine Mukendi and together they have a son named Win Prince Khalala, whose birth was a miracle from God after nice years of marriage.

A licensed Minister since 2005 from All Nations Full Gospel Church International, he was ordained Reverend from Rhema Bible Institute in Toronto, Canada in September 2014.

He has planted two churches in the City of Montreal, Canada, and is a member of the Dunamis International Missionary to Trinidad and other Islands and currently serves as a branch Pastor of the Transforming Life Centre in the city of Montreal.

Khalala has held different ministries in the local church such as usher, worship leader and musician, deacon, prayer pastor and youth Pastor. Pastor Pitchou operates under a great anointing to help people *break* out and *break* through in life. He has such a passion for prayer that if you ever get close to him you will be contaminated.

Pastor Pitchou's messages are revolutionary, causing you to enter into the deeper realms of revelation of the word of God. Under the leadership of Dr. Ralph Dartey, the General Overseer of Transforming Life Centre International, he has been a guest to many conference, crusades and leadership conferences around the world. His passion is to see your life lived according to the mandate of heaven, and build you up to be a type of leader that God has made you to be.

www.ingramcontent.com/pod-product-compliance
Lightning Source LLC
LaVergne TN
LVHW051413080426
835508LV00022B/3070